Poems and Readings for

Weddings and Civil Partnerships

See also the other books in the series:

Poems and Readings for Funeral and Memorials
Compiled by Luisa Moncada

*Poems and Readings for Christenings
and Naming Ceremonies*
Compiled by Susannah Steel

Poems and Readings for

Weddings and Civil Partnerships

Compiled by

A. Vasudevan

Published in 2009 by New Holland Publishers (UK) Ltd
London • Cape Town • Sydney • Auckland
www.newhollandpublishers.com
Garfield House, 86–88 Edgware Road, London W2 2EA, United
Kingdom
80 McKenzie Street, Cape Town 8001, South Africa
Unit 1, 66 Gibbes Street, Chatswood, NSW 2067, Australia
218 Lake Road, Northcote, Auckland, New Zealand

10 9 8 7 6 5 4 3 2 1

Text copyright © A. Vasudevan
Copyright © 2009 New Holland Publishers (UK) Ltd
A. Vasudevan has asserted her moral right to be identified as the
author of this work.
A catalogue record for this book is available from the British Library.
Copyright acknowledgements can be found on pages 188–189

ISBN 978 1 84773 319 1

Publishing Director: Rosemary Wilkinson
Publisher: Aruna Vasudevan
Editor: Julia Shone
Editorial Assistant: Cosima Hibbert
Design: Sarah Williams
Production: Melanie Dowland
DTP: Pete Gwyer
Reproduction by Pica Digital Pte. Ltd., Singapore
Printed and bound in India by Replika Press

The paper used to produce this book is sourced from
sustainable forests.

For Rajama Pillai Vasudevan Nair,
with much love

Contents

Foreword

Choosing suitable readings for your wedding ceremony is arguably one of the most enjoyable or stressful tasks. Being asked to select a reading by a loved one for his or her marriage is also both a great honour and a huge pressure. This book, which brings together around 150 poems and readings from a variety of sources, aims to help make this task much easier.

The readings are arranged alphabetically by author surname and each entry has a tab indicating whether it is a poem, a reading, a song or a spiritual piece or biblical reading. Each poem or extract ends with a short biography of the author. At the back of the book, there is a selection of short and pithy quotations which may also be of use and, for those of us who find it impossible to remember the title or author of things we've read, there is an index arranged by the first line of the selected readings.

We hope you will enjoy the readings and find something suitable to read at either your own or your loved ones' wedding or Civil Partnership. We also hope this makes the job infinitely more enjoyable and one less stress to deal with.

−A. Vasudevan

Choosing a reading

When selecting a reading, there are a number of things to consider:

- Is the reading suitable for the type of ceremony you, your friend or family member is having?
- Has anyone consulted the celebrant or minister for advice?
- Will anyone be offended by the reading you have chosen?
- Will your selection make or break your relationship?

The following may help:

RELIGIOUS CEREMONY

When choosing a reading for a religious wedding ceremony, always make sure that the celebrant or minister has approved your choices. Many people choose to have two readings, one of which is religious. You may be given a selection of readings from the Bible, or the Torah (the ancient Hebrew readings on which the Old Testament is founded), if you are Jewish, but you may also be able to read something secular as well. This could be something that is meaningful to the person or people getting married or words that sum up qualities you or your friend or loved one may possess or deem important. In such cases, it is essential to show the minister/celebrant the reading that has been chosen. Some vicars may, for example, find Shakespeare acceptable, but a poem by someone more contemporary, such as Maya Angelou, may not be allowed.

CIVIL CEREMONIES

If you have chosen to get married in a registry office, readings are not a required part of the ceremony and you must get approval to include them when you marry. If you are getting married in a state-licensed venue, the registrar must approve your choice of reading. When arranging a civil ceremony, please bear in mind that you are not allowed to read anything with religious content and this includes extracts that are considered spiritual or refer to heaven, God, angels or faith – such as Kahlil Gibran's *The Prophet* (*see pages 90–94*).

Other ceremonies, such as a humanist one, for example, may give you more freedom over the kind of readings you can include, or may even give you the opportunity to write and read your own words.

Advice on choosing readings

CHOOSING THE PERFECT BIBLE READING
Although the choice of biblical reading is basically down to you, do check with the church concerned which version of the Bible is commonly used.

DIFFERENT VERSIONS OF THE BIBLE:

- **The King James Version:** This dates back to the 17th century and is considered by some people to be very beautiful. Others consider the language to be outdated and difficult to understand.
- **New International Version (NIV)** is a completely new translation made by over 100 scholars, first published in 1973, which uses a clear, contemporary style of language.
- **The New English Bible (NEB)** or the **Good News Bible** are also up-to-date versions but are sometimes criticised for being slightly mundane.
- **The Anglican Alternative Service Book (ASB)** brings together different versions of readings.
- **New Jerusalem Bible** is used by Roman Catholics. There is also a more gender-inclusive version available.

NON-RELIGIOUS READINGS
These are usually poems or extracts from books or novels that have some particular relevance to the bride or bridegroom. *Poems and Readings for Wedding and Civil Partnerships* includes several extracts from non-religious sources.

If I Speak in the Tongues of Men

1 CORINTHIANS 13:1—13

1 If I speak in the tongues of men and of angels, but have not love, I am only a resounding gong or a clanging cymbal.

2 If I have the gift of prophecy and can fathom all mysteries and all knowledge, and if I have a faith that can move mountains, but have not love, I am nothing.

3 If I give all I possess to the poor and surrender my body to the flames, but have not love, I gain nothing.

4 Love is patient, love is kind. It does not envy, it does not boast, it is not proud.

5 It is not rude, it is not self-seeking, it is not easily angered, it keeps no record of wrongs.

6 Love does not delight in evil but rejoices with the truth.

7 It always protects, always trusts, always hopes, always perseveres.

8 Love never fails. But where there are prophecies, they will cease; where there are tongues, they will be stilled; where there is knowledge, it will pass away.

9 For we know in part and we prophesy in part,

10 but when perfection comes, the imperfect disappears.

11 When I was a child, I talked like a child, I thought like a child, I reasoned like a child. When I became a man, I put childish ways behind me.

12 Now we see but a poor reflection as in a mirror; then we shall see face to face. Now I know in part; then I shall know fully, even as I am fully known.

13 And now these three remain: faith, hope and love. But the greatest of these is love.

New International Version

BIBLICAL

Dear Friends, Let Us Love One Another

1 JOHN 4:7-19

7   Dear friends, let us love one another, for love is from God. Everyone who loves has been born of God and knows God.

8   Whoever does not love does not know God, because God is love.

9   This is how God showed his love among us: He sent his one and only Son into the world that we might live through Him.

10 This is love, not that we loved God, but that He loved us and sent His Son as an atoning sacrifice for our sins.

11 Dear friends, since God so loved us, we also ought to love one another.

12 No one has ever seen God; but if we love one another, God lives in us and His love is made complete in us.

13 We know that we live in Him and He in us, because He has given us of His Spirit.

14 And we have seen and testify that the Father has sent the Son to be the Saviour of the world.

15 If anyone acknowledges that Jesus is the Son of God, God lives in him, and he in God.

16 And so we know and rely on the love God has for us. God is love. Whoever lives in love lives in God, and God in him.

17 In this way, love is made complete among us so that we will have confidence on the day of judgement, because in this world we are like Him.

18 There is no fear in love. But perfect love drives out fear, because fear has to do with punishment. The one who fears is not made perfect in love.

19 We love because He first loved us.

New International Version

Love

READING

DIANE ACKERMAN

Love. What a small word we use for an idea so
immense and powerful. It has altered the flow of
history, calmed monsters, kindled works of art,
cheered the forlorn, turned tough guys to mush,
consoled the enslaved, driven strong women mad,
glorified the humble, fuelled national scandals,
bankrupted robber barons, and made mincemeat
of kings. How can love's spaciousness be conveyed
in the narrow confines of one syllable? Love is an
ancient delirium, a desire older than civilisation,
with taproots spreading into deep and mysterious
days. The heart is a living museum. In each of its
galleries, no matter how narrow or dimly lit,
preserved forever like wondrous diatoms, are our
moments of loving, and being loved.

17

_Diane Ackerman (b. 1948) is an American writer and poet who delights
in crossing boundaries between science, literature and journalism. Love is a
recurring theme and her writing brims with her belief in the power of love._

POEM

Come. And Be My Baby

MAYA ANGELOU

The highway is full of big cars
going nowhere fast
And folks is smoking anything that'll burn
Some people wrap their lives around a cocktail
glass
And you sit wondering
where you're going to turn
I got it.
Come. And be my baby.

Some prophets say the world is gonna end
tomorrow
But others say we've got a week or two
The paper is full of every kind of blooming horror
And you sit wondering
what you're gonna do.
I got it.
Come. And be my baby.

Maya Angelou (b. 1928) is an African American singer, poet, playwright, actor, author, civil rights activist, producer and director, best known for her memoir, I Know Why the Caged Bird Sings.

A Walled Garden

A N O N

'Your marriage', he said, 'Should have within it a secret and protected place, open to you alone. Imagine it to be a walled garden. Entered by a door to which only you have the key. Within this garden you will cease to be a mother, father, employee, homemaker or any other roles which you fulfil in daily life. Here you are yourselves, two people who love each other. Here you can concentrate on one another's needs. So take my hand and let us go back to our garden. The time we spend together is not wasted but invested. Invested in our future and the nurture of our love.'

SPIRITUAL

Apache Blessing

A N O N

Now you will feel no rain, for each of you
will be the shelter for each other. Now you
will feel no cold, for each of you will be the
warmth for the other. Now you are two
persons, but there is only one life before.
Go now to your dwelling place to enter
into the days of your life together. And may
your days be good and long upon the earth.

Treat yourself and each other with respect,
and remind yourselves often of what brought
you together. Give the highest priority to
the tenderness, gentleness and kindness that
your connection deserves. When frustration,
difficulty and fear assail your relationship –
as they threaten all relationships at one time
or another – remember to focus on what is
right between you, not only the part which
seems wrong. In this way, you can ride out
the storms when clouds hide the face of the
sun in your lives – remembering that even if
you lose sight of it for a moment, the sun is still
there. And if each of you takes responsibility
for the quality of your life together, it will be
marked by abundance and delight.

Chinese Poem

A N O N

I want to be your friend
Forever and ever
When the hills are all flat
And the rivers run dry
When the trees blossom in winter
And the snow falls in summer,
When heaven and earth mix
Not till then will I part from you.

from A Native American Wedding Ceremony

ANON

May the sun bring you new happiness by day;
May the moon softly restore you by night;
May the rain wash away your worries
And the breeze blow new strength into your being,
And all the days of your life
May you walk gently through the world
And know its beauty.
Now you will feel no rain,
For each of you will be warmth for the other.
Now there will be no more loneliness.

From This Day Forward

ANON

From this day forward,
You shall not walk alone.
My heart will be your shelter,
And my arms will be your home.

Hawaiian Song

A N O N

Here all seeking is over,
the lost has been found,
a mate has been found
to share the chills of winter –
now Love asks
that you be united.

Here is a place to rest,
a place to sleep,
a place in heaven.
Now two are becoming one,
the black night is scattered,
the eastern sky grows bright.
At last the great day has come!

I Knew that I had been Touched by Love

ANON

I knew that I had been touched by love the
first time I saw you, and I felt your warmth,
and I heard your laughter. I knew that I had
been touched by love when I was hurting from
something that happened, and you came along
and made the hurt go away. I knew that I had
been touched by love when I stopped making
plans with my friends, and started dreaming
dreams with you. I knew that I had been touched
by love when I suddenly stopped thinking in
terms of 'me' and started thinking in terms
of 'we'. I knew that I had been touched by love
when suddenly I couldn't make decisions by
myself anymore, and I had the strong desire to
share everything with you. I knew that I had
been touched by love the first time we spent
alone together, and I knew that I wanted to
stay with you forever because I had never felt
this touched by love.

Irish Blessing

ANON

May the road rise to meet you,
May the wind be always at your back,
May the sun shine warm upon your face,
The rains fall soft upon your fields.
And until we meet again,
May God hold you in the palm of his hand.

May God be with you and bless you;
May you see your children's children.
May you be poor in misfortune,
Rich in blessings,
May you know nothing but happiness
From this day forward.

May the road rise to meet you,
May the wind be always at your back,
May the warm rays of sun fall upon your home
And may the hand of a friend always be near.

May green be the grass you walk on,
May blue be the skies above you,
May pure be the joys that surround you,
May true be the hearts that love you.

The Key to Love

ANON, 1ST—CENTURY CHINA

The key to love is understanding ...
The ability to comprehend not only the spoken word,
but those unspoken gestures,
the little things that say so much by themselves.

The key to love is forgiveness ...
to accept each other's faults and pardon mistakes,
without forgetting, but with remembering
what you learn from them.

The key to love is sharing ...
Facing your good fortunes as well as the bad, together;
both conquering problems, forever searching for ways
to intensify your happiness.

The key to love is giving ...
without thought of return,
but with the hope of just a simple smile,
and by giving in but never giving up.

The key to love is respect ...
realising that you are two separate people, with different ideas;
that you don't belong to each other,
that you belong with each other, and share a mutual bond.

The key to love is inside us all ...
It takes time and patience to unlock all the ingredients
that will take you to its threshold;
it is the continual learning process that demands a lot of work ...
but the rewards are more than worth the effort ...
and that is the key to love.

These I Can Promise

ANON

I cannot promise you a life of sunshine;
I cannot promise riches, wealth, or gold;
I cannot promise you an easy pathway
That leads away from change or growing old.

But I can promise all my heart's devotion;
A smile to chase away your tears of sorrow;
A love that's ever true and ever growing;
A hand to hold in yours through each tomorrow.

True Love

POEM

ANON

True love is a sacred flame
That burns eternally,
And none can dim its special glow
Or change its destiny.
True love speaks in tender tones
And hears with gentle ear,
True love gives with open heart
And true love conquers fear.
True love makes no harsh demands
It neither rules nor binds,
And true love holds with gentle hands
The hearts that it entwines.

The Promises of Marriage

ANON

Marriage is a promise of companionship,
Of having someone to share
All of life's experiences.

Marriage does not promise that there will
Not be any rough times,
Just the assurance that there will
Always be someone
Who cares and will help you through
To better times.

Marriage does not promise eternal romance,
Just eternal love and commitment.
Marriage cannot prevent disappointments,
Disillusionment, or grief,
But it can offer hope, acceptance,
And comfort.

Marriage can't protect you from making
Individual choices
Or shelter you from the world,
But it will help to reassure you
That there is someone by your side
Who truly cares.

When the world hurts you
And makes you feel vulnerable,

Marriage offers the promise that there will
Be someone waiting to listen,
To console, to inspire.

Marriage is the joining of two people
Who share the promise
That only marriage can make –
To share the sunshine and the shadows,
And to experience a richer, more fulfilling life
Because of it.

Women:
Look, Listen and Take Heed!

ANON

Have dinner ready. Plan ahead, even the night before, to have a delicious meal ready on time for his return. This is a way of letting him know that you have been thinking about him and are concerned about his needs.

Most men are hungry when they come home and the prospect of a good meal (especially his favourite dish) is part of the warm welcome needed.

Prepare yourself: take 15 minutes to rest so you'll be refreshed when he arrives. Touch up your make-up, put a ribbon in your hair and be fresh-looking. He has just been with a lot of work weary people.

Be a little gay and a little more interesting for him. His boring day may need a lift and one of your duties is to provide it. Clear away the clutter. Make one last trip through the main part of the house just before your husband arrives. Gather up school books, toys, paper etc. and then run a dust cloth over the tables.

Over the cooler months of the year you should prepare and light a fire for him to unwind by. Your husband will feel he has reached a haven of rest and order, and it will give you a lift too. After all, catering for his comfort will provide you with immense personal satisfaction.

Prepare the children, take a few minutes to wash their hands and faces (if they are small), comb their hair, and if necessary, change their clothes. They are little treasures and he would like to see them playing the part.

Minimise all noise. At the time of his arrival, eliminate all noise from the washer, dryer, and vacuum. Try to encourage the children to be quiet. Be happy to see him. Greet him with a warm smile and show sincerity in your desire to see him.

Listen to him. You may have a dozen important things to tell him, but the moment of his arrival is not the time. Let him talk first. Remember, his topics of conversation are more important than yours.

Make the evening his. Never complain if he comes home late or goes out to dinner or other places of entertainment without you. Instead try to understand his world of strain and pressure, and his very real need to be at home and relax.

Your goal. Try to make sure your home is a place of peace, order and tranquillity where your husband can renew himself in body and spirit. Don't greet him with complaints and problems. Don't complain if he's late for dinner or even if he stays out all night. Count this as minor compared to what he might have gone through that day.

Make him comfortable. Have him lean back in a comfortable chair or have him lie down in the bedroom. Have a cool or warm drink ready for him. Arrange his pillow and offer to take off his shoes. Speak in a low soothing and pleasant voice. Don't ask him questions about his actions or question his judgement or integrity.

Remember, he is the master of the house and as such will always exercise his will with fairness and truthfulness. You have no right to question him.

A good wife always knows her place.

An extract possibly taken directly from a 1950s home economics text book titled The Good Wives Guide.

33

POEM

Somewhere

SIR EDWIN ARNOLD

Somewhere there waiteth in this world of ours
For one lone soul another lonely soul,
Each choosing each through all the weary hours
And meeting strangely at one sudden goal.
Then blend they, like green leaves with golden flowers,
Into one beautiful and perfect whole;
And life's long night is ended, and the way
Lies open onward to eternal day.

Sir Edwin Arnold (1832–1904) was a British author and journalist. He was editor of the Daily Telegraph *between 1873 and 1888. Arnold is most famous for his blank verse epic,* The Light of Asia, *which examined the life of Buddha.*

Habitation

MARGARET ATWOOD

Marriage is not
a house or even a tent

it is before that, and colder:

the edge of the forest, the edge
of the desert
the unpainted stairs
at the back where we squat
outside, eating popcorn

the edge of the receding glacier

where painfully and with wonder
at having survived even
this far

we are learning to make fire

Margaret Atwood (b. 1939) is an award-winning Canadian author. She has written more than 40 books including novels, short stories, literary criticism, social history, books for children and poetry. She has been writing for over 35 years, during which time she has received numerous awards.

POEM

Lullaby

W.H. AUDEN

Lay your sleeping head, my love,
Human on my faithless arm:
Time and fevers burn away
Individual beauty from
Thoughtful children, and the grave
Proves the child ephemeral:
But in my arms till break of day
Let the living creature lie,
Mortal, guilty, but to me
The entirely beautiful.

Soul and body have no bounds:
To lovers as they lie upon
Her tolerant enchanted slope
In their ordinary swoon,
Grave the vision Venus sends
Of supernatural sympathy,
Universal love and hope;
While an abstract insight wakes
Among the glaciers and the rocks
The hermit's carnal ecstasy.

Certainty, fidelity
On the stroke of midnight pass
Like vibrations of a bell
And fashionable madmen raise
Their pedantic boring cry:

Every farthing of the cost,
All the dreaded cards foretell,
Shall be paid, but from this night
Not a whisper, not a thought,
Not a kiss nor look be lost.

Beauty, midnight, vision dies:
Let the winds of dawn that blow
Softly round your dreaming head
Such a day of welcome show
Eye and knocking heart may bless,
Find our mortal world enough;
Noons of dryness find you fed
By the involuntary powers,
Nights of insult let you pass
Watched by every human love.

W. H. Auden (1907–1973) is probably one of the best-known English poets of the 20th Century. His first book, Poems, *was published when he was only 23; it was followed by further volumes of poetry and plays. Auden is acknowledged as a master of verse, and his influence on modern poetry has been immense.*

O Tell Me the Truth about Love

W.H. AUDEN

Some say that love's a little boy,
And some say it's a bird,
Some say it makes the world go around,
And some say that's absurd,
And when I asked the man next-door,
Who looked as if he knew,
His wife got very cross indeed,
And said it wouldn't do.

Does it look like a pair of pyjamas,
Or the ham in a temperance hotel?
Does its odour remind one of llamas,
Or has it a comforting smell?
Is it prickly to touch as a hedge is,
Or soft as eiderdown fluff?
Is it sharp or quite smooth at the edges?
O tell me the truth about love.

Our history books refer to it
In cryptic little notes,
It's quite a common topic on
The Transatlantic boats;
I've found the subject mentioned in
Accounts of suicides,
And even seen it scribbled on
The backs of railway guides.

Does it howl like a hungry Alsatian,
Or boom like a military band?
Could one give a first-rate imitation
On a saw or a Steinway Grand?

Is its singing at parties a riot?
Does it only like Classical stuff?
Will it stop when one wants to be quiet?
O tell me the truth about love.

I looked inside the summer-house;
It wasn't over there;
I tried the Thames at Maidenhead,
And Brighton's bracing air.
I don't know what the blackbird sang,
Or what the tulip said;
But it wasn't in the chicken-run,
Or underneath the bed.

Can it pull extraordinary faces?
Is it usually sick on a swing?
Does it spend all its time at the races,
Or fiddling with pieces of string?
Has it views of its own about money?
Does it think Patriotism enough?
Are its stories vulgar but funny?
O tell me the truth about love.

When it comes, will it come without warning
Just as I'm picking my nose?
Will it knock on my door in the morning,
Or tread in the bus on my toes?
Will it come like a change in the weather?
Will its greeting be courteous or rough?
Will it alter my life altogether?
O tell me the truth about love.

POEM

Yes, I'll Marry You, my Dear

PAM AYRES

Yes, I'll marry you, my dear, and here's the reason why;
So I can push you out of bed when the baby starts to cry,
And if we hear a knocking and it's creepy and it's late,
I hand you the torch you see, and you investigate.

Yes I'll marry you, my dear, you may not apprehend it,
But when the tumble-drier goes it's you that has to mend it,
You have to face the neighbour, should our labrador attack him,
And if a drunkard fondles me, it's you that has to whack him.

Yes, I'll marry you, you're virile and you're lean,
My house is like a pigsty, you can help to keep it clean.
That sexy little dinner which you served by candlelight,
As I do chipolatas, you can cook it every night!

It's you who has to work the drill and put up curtain track,
And when I've got PMT it's you who gets the flak,
I do see great advantages, but none of them for you,
And so before you see the light, I do, I do, I do!

40

Pam Ayres (b. 1947) is a comic poet. She often appears on radio and TV and has been voted one of the funniest women in Britain several times.

If Thou Must Love Me

ELIZABETH BARRETT BROWNING

If thou must love me, let it be for naught
Except for love's sake only. Do not say,
'I love her for her smile – her look – her way
Of speaking gently, for a trick of thought
That falls in well with mine, and certes brought
A sense of pleasant ease on such a day' –
For these things in themselves, Beloved, may
Be changed, or change for thee – and love, so wrought,
May be unwrought so. Neither love me for
Thine own dear pity's wiping my cheeks dry:
A creature might forget to weep, who bore
Thy comfort long, and lose thy love thereby!
But love me for love's sake, that evermore
Thou may'st love on, through love's eternity.

*Elizabeth Barrett Browning (1806–1861) is among the greatest
contributors to English poetry. Much of her writing was inspired by her love for
her husband, Robert Browning; the collection,* Sonnets From the Portuguese,
is a collection of love sonnets written during their courtship.

POEM

from Sonnets from the Portuguese

Elizabeth Barrett Browning

How do I love thee? Let me count the ways.
I love thee to the depth and breadth and height
My soul can reach, when feeling out of sight
For the ends of Being and ideal Grace.
I love thee to the level of every day's
Most quiet need, by sun and candlelight.
I love thee freely, as men strive for Right;
I love thee purely, as they turn from Praise.
I love thee with the passion put to use
In my old griefs, and with my childhood's faith.
I love thee with a love I seemed to lose
With my lost saints, – I love thee with the breath,
Smiles, tears, of all my life! – and, if God choose,
I shall but love thee better after death.

from Love Letters between Robert and Elizabeth Barrett Browning

To Elizabeth Barrett Browning:

... would I, if I could, supplant one of any of the affections
that I know to have taken root in you – that great and
solemn one, for instance.

I feel that if I could get myself remade, as if turned to gold,
I would not even then desire to become more than
the mere setting to that diamond you must always wear.

The regard and esteem you now give me, in this letter,
and which I press to my heart and bow my head upon,
is all I can take and all too embarrassing, using all
my gratitude.

To Robert Browning:

And now listen to me in turn. You have touched me more
profoundly than I thought even you could have touched
me – my heart was full when you came here today.
Henceforward I am yours for everything....

POEM

Life in a Love

ROBERT BROWNING

Escape me?
Never –
Beloved!
While I am I, and you are you,
So long as the world contains us both,
Me the loving and you the loth,
While the one eludes, must the other pursue.
My life is a fault at last, I fear:
It seems too much like a fate, indeed!
Though I do my best I shall scarce succeed.
But what if I fail of my purpose here?
It is but to keep the nerves at strain,
To dry one's eyes and laugh at a fall,
And, baffled, get up and begin again, –
So the chase takes up one's life, that's all.
While, look but once from your farthest bound
At me so deep in the dust and dark,
No sooner the old hope goes to ground
Than a new one, straight to the selfsame mark,
I shape me –
Ever
Removed!

Robert Browning (1812–1889) was a renowned English poet and playwright.

Have You Ever

JODY BECK

Have you ever just met a person
Who made your head turn
Have you ever met a person
Who made your heart burn
Have you ever met a person
That let you be you
Have you ever met a person
That made you feel love true
Have you ever met a person
Who touched you so deep
Have you ever met a person
Without whom you could not sleep

Have you ever met a person
That brightened your life
Have you ever met a person
That made you want to be a wife
Have you ever met a person
Whose eyes promise you'll never feel blue
I know you have
Because that person is you.

Love Letters

LUDWIG VAN BEETHOVEN TO THE
'IMMORTAL BELOVED'

July 6, 1806

Even when I am in bed my thoughts rush to you, my eternally beloved, now and then joyfully, then again sadly, waiting to know whether Fate will hear our prayer – To face life I must live altogether with you or never see you. Yes, I am resolved to be a wanderer abroad until I can fly to your arms and say that I have found my true home with you and enfolded in your arms can let my soul be wafted to the realm of blessed spirits – alas, unfortunately it must be so – You will become composed, the more so you know that I am faithful to you; no other woman can ever possess my heart – never – never – Oh God, why must one be separated form her who is so dear. Yet my life in V[ienna] at present is a miserable life – Your love has made me both the happiest and the unhappiest of mortals – At my age I now need stability and regularity in my life – can this coexist with our relationship? – Angel, I have just heard that the post goes every day – and therefore I must close, so that you may receive the letter immediately – Be calm; for only by calmly considering our lives can we achieve our purpose to live together – Be calm – love me – Today – yesterday – what tearful longing for you – for you – you – my life – my all – all good wishes to you – Oh, do continue to love me – never misjudge your lover's most faithful heart.

> ever yours
> ever mine
> ever ours.

Ludwig van Beethoven (1770–1827) was one of the greatest composers of the 19th century. The 'Immortal Beloved' referred to in this letter remains unidentified; indeed the letter was only discovered after Beethoven's death.

My Lady Love

ROBERT C.O. BENJAMIN

There are none so happy as my love and I,
None so joyous, blithe and free;
The reason is, that I love her,
And the reason is, she loves me.

There are none so sweet as my own fond love,
None so beauteous or true;
Her equal I could never find,
Though I search the whole world thro'.

There's no love so true as my lady sweet;
None so constant to its troth;
There's naught on earth like her so dear,
No queen her equal in her worth.

So there's none so happy as my love and I;
None so blissful, blithe and free,
And the reason is that I am hers,
And she, in truth, belongs to me.

Robert C. O. Benjamin (1855–1900) studied law at Trinity College in Oxford, Virginia. He was editor of the Negro American *in Birmingham, Alabama, and he owned and edited the* Colored Citizen *in Pittsburgh and the* Chronicle *in Evansville, Indiana. He is believed to have been the first black lawyer in California.*

from A Love Letter to Josephine

NAPOLEON BONAPARTE

April 3, 1796

... My one and only Josephine, apart from you there is no joy; away from you, the world is a desert where I am alone and cannot open my heart. You have taken more than my soul; you are the one thought of my life.

When I am tired of the worry of work, when I feel the outcome, when men annoy me, when I am ready to curse being alive, I put my hand on my heart; your portrait hangs there, I look at it, and love brings me perfect happiness, and all is miling except the time I must spend away from my mistress.

By what art have you captivated all my facilities and concentrated my whole being in you? It is a sweet friend, that will die only when I do.

... Oh, my adorable wife! I don't know what fate has in store for me, but if it keeps me apart from you any longer, it will be unbearable! My courage is not enough for that.

... I used often to say men cannot harm one who dies without regret; but, now, to die not loved by you, to die without knowing, would be the torment of Hell, the living image of utter desolation. I feel I am suffocating.

My one companion, you whom fate has destined to travel the sorry road of life beside me, the day I lose your heart will be the day Nature loses warmth and life for me ...

48

Napoleon Bonaparte (1769–1821) was one of the greatest military leaders in history and, as emperor of France, he conquered much of Europe. The Battle of Waterloo, in June 1815, ended his reign and he was imprisoned on the remote Atlantic island of St. Helena, where he died on 5 May 1821.

from A Wedding Sermon from a Prison Cell

READING

DIETRICH BONHOEFFER,

It is right and proper for a bride and bridegroom to welcome and celebrate their wedding day with a unique sense of triumph. When all the difficulties, obstacles, hindrances, doubts, and misgivings have been, not made light of, but honestly faced and overcome – and it is certainly better not to take everything for granted – then both parties have indeed achieved the most important triumph of their lives. With the 'Yes' that they have said to each other, they have by their free choice given a new direction to their lives; they have cheerfully and confidently defied all the uncertainties and hesitations with which, as they know, a lifelong partnership between two people is faced; and by their own free and responsible action they have conquered a new land to live in. Every wedding must be an occasion of joy that human beings can do such great things, that they have been given such immense freedom and power to take the helm in their life's journey. The children of the earth are rightly proud of being allowed to take a hand in shaping their own destinies, and something of this pride must contribute to the happiness of a bride and bridegroom....

Dietrich Bonhoeffer (1906–1945) was a theologian and spiritual adviser, prominent in the Protestant Church's fight against the Nazi government. He wrote the above while in Tegel Prison, Berlin, in May 1943. It was written to his niece, Renate, and a boy from the neighbourhood.

POEM

To my Dear and Loving Husband

ANNE BRADSTREET

If ever two were one, then surely we.
If ever man were loved by wife, then thee;
If ever wife was happy in a man,
Compare with me ye women if you can.
I prize thy love more than whole mines of gold,
Or all the riches that the East doth hold.
My love is such that rivers cannot quench,
Nor ought but love from thee give recompense.
Thy love is such I can no way repay,
The heavens reward thee manifold, I pray.
Then while we live, in love let's so persevere,
That when we live no more, we may live ever.

Anne Bradstreet (c.1612–1672) was among the first Puritan emigrants to America in the 1630s. She wrote poetry, mainly based on her own experiences and her love for her husband and family. Bradstreet's religious devotion is clear, as is her dedication to free thought, intellect and knowledge.

Because She Would Ask Me Why I Loved Her

CHRISTOPHER BRENNAN

POEM

If questioning would make us wise
No eyes would ever gaze in eyes;
If all our tale were told in speech
No mouths would wander each to each.

Were spirits free from mortal mesh
And love not bound in hearts of flesh
No aching breasts would yearn to meet
And find their ecstasy complete.

For who is there that lives and knows
The secret powers by which he grows?
Were knowledge all, what were our need
To thrill and faint and sweetly bleed?

Then seek not, sweet, the 'If' and 'Why'
I love you now until I die.
For I must love because I live
And life in me is what you give.

51

Christopher Brennan (1870–1932) was a poet and scholar. Unhappily married, he fell in love with Violet Singer and, after her sudden death, wrote some of his finest poetry.

POEM

My Delight and Thy Delight

ROBERT BRIDGES

My delight and thy delight
Walking, like two angels white,
In the gardens of the night:

My desire and thy desire
Twining to a tongue of fire,
Leaping live, and laughing higher:

Thro' the everlasting strife
In the mysteries of life.
Love, from whom the world begun,
Hath the secret of the sun.

Love can tell, and love alone,
Whence the million stars were strewn,
Why each atom knows its own,
How, in spite of woe and death,
Gay is life, and sweet is breath:

This he taught us, this we knew,
Happy in his science true,
Hand in hand as we stood
'Neath the shadows of the wood,
Heart to heart as we lay
In the dawning of the day.

Robert Bridges (1844–1930) was born in Kent, England, and educated at Eton College and the University of Oxford. He was Poet Laureate from 1913 onwards, but he only achieved great fame near the end of his life. He is renowned for his poetry's precision whilst also holding great strength of expression.

from Sermon at Rajagaha

BUDDHA

Do not deceive, do not despise each other anywhere.
Do not be angry, nor bear secret resentments;
for as a mother will risk her life and watches over her child,
so boundless be your love to all, so tender, kind and mild.

Cherish good will right and left, early and late, and without
hindrance, without stint, be free of hate and envy, while standing
and walking and sitting down, what ever you have in mind,
the rule of life that is always best is to be loving-kind.

Gifts are great, founding temples is meritorious,
meditations and religious exercises pacify the heart,
comprehension of the truth leads to Nirvana,
but greater than all is loving kindness.

As the light of the moon is 16 times stronger than the light
of all the stars, so loving kindness is 16 times more efficacious
in liberating the heart than all other religious accomplishments
taken together.

*Siddhartha Buddha (b. 560BC) was born a prince in Lumbini, Nepal.
When he was a young man he escaped the palace of his birth and became the
Buddha, the enlightened one, whose teachings of wisdom and enlightenment
were to become the foundations of Buddhism.*

A Red, Red Rose

ROBERT BURNS

O my Luve's like a red, red rose,
That's newly sprung in June;
O my Luve's like the melodie
That's sweetly play'd in tune.

As fair art thou, my bonie lass,
So deep in luve am I;
And I will luve thee still, my Dear,
Till a' the seas gang dry.

Till a' the seas gang dry, my Dear,
And the rocks melt wi' the sun:
I will luve thee still, my Dear,
While the sands o' life shall run.

And fare thee weel, my only Luve!
And fare thee weel, a while!
And I will come again, my Luve,
Tho' it were ten thousand mile.

*Robert Burns (1759–1796) is the national poet of Scotland. Together with Sir
Walter Scott he created an enduring Scottish identity at a time when the Scots might
have been entirely absorbed into a general British culture. In particular, Burns
preserved the Scots tongue in literary form.*

So, We'll Go No More A-roving

POEM

LORD BYRON

So, we'll go no more a-roving
So late into the night,
Though the heart be still as loving,
And the moon be still as bright.

For the sword outweighs its sheath,
And the soul wears out the breast,
And the heart must pause to breathe,
And love itself have rest.

Though the night was made for loving,
And the day returns too soon,
Yet we'll go no more a-roving,
By the light of the moon.

Lord Byron (George Gordon Noel Byron; 1788–1824) was a London-born poet and famous society figure. The 'Byronic hero', a defiant, melancholy young man, brooding on some mysterious, unforgivable event in his past, was characterised by Lord Byron.

When We Two Parted

LORD BYRON

When we two parted
In silence and tears,
Half broken-hearted
To sever the years,
Pale grew thy cheek and cold,
Colder, thy kiss;
Truly that hour foretold
Sorrow to this.

The dew of the morning
Sunk, chill on my brow,
It felt like the warning
Of what I feel now.
Thy vows are all broken,
And light is thy fame;
I hear thy name spoken,
And share in its shame.

They name thee before me,
A knell to mine ear;
A shudder comes o'er me...
Why wert thou so dear?
They know not I knew thee,
Who knew thee too well...
Long, long shall I rue thee,
Too deeply to tell.

In secret we met
In silence I grieve
That thy heart could forget,
Thy spirit deceive.
If I should meet thee
After long years,
How should I greet thee?
With silence and tears.

POEM

Forgive Me but I Needs Must Press

ALICE CARY

Forgive me, but I needs must press
One question, since I love you so;
And kiss me, darling, if it's Yes,
And, darling, kiss me if it's No!

It is about our marriage day,
I fain would have it even here;
But kiss me if it's far away,
And, darling, kiss me if it's near!

Ah, by the blushes crowding so
On cheek and brow, 'tis near, I guess;
But, darling, kiss me if it's No,
And kiss me, darling, if it's Yes!

And with what flowers shall you be wed?
With flowers of snow? Or flowers of flame?
But be they white, or be they red,
Kiss me, my darling, all the same!

And have you sewed your wedding dress?
Nay, speak not, even whisper low;
But kiss me, darling, if it's Yes,
And, darling, kiss me if it's No!

Alice Cary (1820–1871) was an idealistic and moralistic American poet. She had a passion for justice and hated oppression of any kind. Both Cary and her sister, Phoebe, were determined to make a career in writing, surviving on the small income that their poems and short stories provided.

Garland your Hair with Majoram

CATULLUS

Garland your hair with majoram
Soft-scented; veil your face and come smiling down to us,
Saffron shoes on milk-white feet.
Awakened on this happy day,
Join us in lusty marriage songs
Join us in dancing, holding high
The marriage torch

Catullus (c. 84–54BC) belonged to a circle of neoteroi *(new poets), who wrote elegant and allusive poems on subjects such as love, friendship and myth. Catullus is renowned for sensous and passionate writing about his intense love affair with Clodia, the wife of Metellus Celer, whom he refers to as 'Lesbia'.*

POEM

Love Lives

JOHN CLARE

Love lives beyond
The tomb, the earth, which fades like dew.
I love the fond,
The faithful, and the true

Love lives in sleep,
The happiness of healthy dreams
Eve's dews may weep,
But love delightful seems.

'Tis heard in spring
When light and sunbeams, warm and kind,
On angels' wing
Bring love and music to the mind.

And where is voice,
So young, so beautiful and sweet
As nature's choice,
Where Spring and lovers meet?

Love lives beyond
The tomb, the earth, the flowers, and dew.
I love the fond,
The faithful, young and true.

John Clare (1793–1864), known as the 'Northamptonshire Peasant Poet', achieved brief popularity during the London vogue for rustic poets in the early 19th century. His life was one of sadness: his first love, Mary Joyce, was forbidden to see him due to his class, and this loss pervades his writing.

First Love

JOHN CLARE

I ne'er was struck before that hour
With love so sudden and so sweet,
Her face it bloomed like a sweet flower
And stole my heart away complete.
My face turned pale as deadly pale.
My legs refused to walk away,
And when she looked, what could I ail?
My life and all seemed turned to clay.

And then my blood rushed to my face
And took my eyesight quite away,
The trees and bushes round the place
Seemed midnight at noonday.
I could not see a single thing,
Words from my eyes did start --
They spoke as chords do from the string,
And blood burnt round my heart.

Are flowers the winter's choice?
Is love's bed always snow?
She seemed to hear my silent voice,
Not love's appeals to know.
I never saw so sweet a face
As that I stood before.
My heart has left its dwelling-place
And can return no more.

POEM

The Presence of Love

SAMUEL TAYLOR COLERIDGE

And in Life's noisiest hour,
There whispers still the ceaseless Love of Thee,
The heart's Self-solace and soliloquy.

You mould my Hopes, you fashion me within;
And to the leading Love-throb in the Heart
Thro' all my Being, thro' my pulse's beat;
You lie in all my many Thoughts, like Light,
Like the fair light of Dawn, or summer Eve
On rippling Stream, or cloud-reflecting Lake.
And looking to the Heaven, that bends above you,
How oft! I bless the Lot that made me love you.

Samuel Taylor Coleridge (1772–1834) was a visionary poet. Coleridge's friendship with poet William Wordsworth was one of the most fruitful relationships in English literary history and their joint publication of Lyrical Ballads, *in 1798, is seen as the starting point for the English Romantic Movement.*

Friendship

POEM

HARTLEY COLERIDGE

When we were idlers with the loitering rills,
The need of human love we little noted:
Our love was nature; and the peace that floated
On the white mist, and dwelt upon the hills,
To sweet accord subdued our wayward wills:
One soul was ours, one mind, one heart devoted,
That, wisely doting, ask'd not why it doted,
And ours the unknown joy, which knowing kills.
But now I find how dear thou wert to me;
That man is more than half of nature's treasure,
Of that fair beauty which no eye can see,
Of that sweet music which no ear can measure;
And now the streams may sing for others' pleasure,
The hills sleep on in their eternity.

Hartley Coleridge (1796–1849), the eldest son of Samuel Taylor Coleridge gained a fellowship to Oriel college, Oxford. He published a small volume of poems, which established his literary reputation, in 1833. After his death, Coleridge's brother, Derwent, published the remainder of Coleridge's literary works in 1851.

SONG

I Wanna Be Yours

JOHN COOPER CLARKE

I wanna be your vacuum cleaner
breathing in your dust
I wanna be your ford cortina
I will never rust

If you like your coffee hot
let me be your coffee pot
You call the shots
I wanna be yours

I wanna be your raincoat
for those frequent rainy days
I wanna be your dreamboat
when you want to sail away

Let me be your teddy bear
take me with you anywhere
I don't care
I wanna be yours

I wanna be your electric meter
I will not run out
I wanna be the electric heater
you'll get cold without

I wanna be your setting lotion
hold your hair in deep devotion
Deep as the deep Atlantic ocean
that's how deep is my devotion.

I wanna be yours.

John Cooper Clarke (b. 1949) is a performance poet from Salford, England, known as the Bard of Salford. He is often referred to as a punk poet, having gained recognition in the late 1970s amidst the punk movement and has performed as an opening act for such bands as The Sex Pistols, Buzzcocks and Elvis Costello.

POEM

After the Lunch

WENDY COPE

On Waterloo Bridge where we said our goodbyes,
the weather conditions bring tears to my eyes.
I wipe them away with a black woolly glove
And try not to notice I've fallen in love.

On Waterloo Bridge I am trying to think:
This is nothing, you're high on the charm and the drink.
But the juke-box inside me is playing a song
That says something different. And when was it wrong?

On Waterloo Bridge with the wind in my hair
I am tempted to skip. You're a fool. I don't care.
the head does its best but the heart is the boss --
I admit it before I am halfway across.

Wendy Cope (b. 1945) was a primary school teacher before her rise to fame as a poet. Her first collection of poems, Making Cocoa for Kingsley Amis, *was published in 1986. She is known for her keen eye for the everyday aspects of English life, most particularly the desires, hopes and frustrations in relationships.*

i carry your heart with me(i carry it in*

E.E. CUMMINGS

POEM

i carry your heart with me(i carry it in
my heart)i am never without it(anywhere
i go you go,my dear;and whatever is done
by only me is your doing,my darling)
                                        i fear
no fate(for you are my fate,my sweet)i want
no world(for beautiful you are my world,my true)
and it's you are whatever a moon has always meant
and whatever a sun will always sing is you

here is the deepest secret nobody knows
(here is the root of the root and the bud of the bud
and the sky of the sky of a tree called life;which grows
higher than soul can hope or mind can hide)
and this is the wonder that's keeping the stars apart

i carry your heart(i carry it in my heart)

* The punctuation and spacing used represents the author's original manuscript.

67

E. E. Cummings (1894–1962) was an American poet known for his experimental style. He visually shaped poems, using a unique and personal grammar and breaking up and putting together words. He often tied this to a traditional and romantic subject matter.

POEM

i love you much(most beautiful darling)*

E.E. CUMMINGS

i love you much(most beautiful darling)

more than anyone on the earth and i
like you better than everything in the sky

—sunlight and singing welcome your coming

although winter may be everywhere
with such a silence and such a darkness
noone can quite begin to guess

(except my life)the true time of year—

and if what calls itself a world should have
the luck to hear such singing(or glimpse such
sunlight as will leap higher than high
through gayer than gayest someone's heart at your each

nearness)everyone certainly would(my
most beautiful darling)believe in nothing but love

* The punctuation and spacing used represents the author's original manuscript.

I Will be Here

STEVEN CURTIS CHAPMAN

Tomorrow morning if you wake
up and the sun does not appear
I will be here
If in the dark, we lose sight of love
Hold my hand, and have no fear
'Cause I will be here

I will be here
When you feel like being quiet
When you need to speak your mind
I will listen
And I will be here
When the laughter turns to cryin'
Through the winning, losing and trying
We'll be together
I will be here

Tomorrow morning, if you wake up
And the future is unclear
I will be here
Just as sure as seasons were made for change
Our lifetimes were made for these years
So I will be here

I will be here
And you can cry on my shoulder
When the mirror tells us we're older
I will hold you
And I will be here
To watch you grow in beauty
And tell you all the things you are to me
I will be here

I will be true to the promise I have made
To you and to the One who gave you to me

Tomorrow morning, if you wake up
And the sun does not appear
I will be here
Oh, I will be here

Steven Curtis Chapman (b. 1962) has been one of the most prominent performers of contemporary Christian music since the 1980s. In his music he often explores themes of love, not only looking at falling in love, but also at relationships and the trials and rewards of loving others.

from The Irrational Season

MADELEINE D'ENGLE

But ultimately there comes a moment when a decision must be made. Ultimately two people who love each other must ask themselves how much they hope for as their love grows and deepens, and how much risk they are willing to take ... It is indeed a fearful gamble ... Because it is the nature of love to create, a marriage itself is something which has to be created, so that, together we become a new creature.

To marry is the biggest risk in human relations that a person can take ... If we commit ourselves to one person for life this is not, as many people think, a rejection of freedom; rather it demands the courage to move into all the risks of freedom, and the risk of love which is permanent; into that love which is not possession, but participation ... It takes a lifetime to learn another person ... When love is not possession, but participation, then it is part of that co-creation which is our human calling, and which implies such risk that it is often rejected.

Madeleine D'Engle (1918–2007) is the author of numerous plays, poems, novels and autobiographies that have entranced both children and adults. She wrote over 60 books and worked as a librarian at the Cathedral Church of St. John the Divine in New York for 30 years.

from The Divine Comedy

DANTE

The love of God, unutterable and perfect,
flows into a pure soul the way light rushes
into a transparent object. The more love we
receive, the more love we shine forth; so
that, as we grow clear and open, the more
complete the joy of loving is. And the more
souls who resonate together, the greater
the intensity of their love for, mirror-like,
each soul reflects the other.

Dante Alighieri (1265–1321) wrote La Divina Commedia *(The Divine Comedy) between 1307 and 1321. It is divided into three parts,* Inferno, Purgatorio *and* Paradiso *and is an allegory of life and God as revealed to a pilgrim.*

Song

C . D A Y L E W I S

Come, live with me and be my love,
And we will all the pleasures prove
Of peace and plenty, bed and board,
That chance employment may afford.

I'll handle dainties on the docks
And thou shalt read of summer frocks:
At evening by the sour canals
We'll hope to hear some madrigals.

Care on thy maiden brow shall put
A wreath of wrinkles, and thy foot
Be shod with pain: not silken dress
But toil shall tire thy loveliness.

Hunger shall make thy modest zone
And cheat fond death of all but bone --
If these delights thy mind may move,
Then live with me and be my love.

*C. Day Lewis (1904–1972) was a poet, essayist and occasional author
of detective fiction. He was appointed Poet Laureate in 1968 and died just
four years later. This poem is a play on Christopher Marlowe's 'The Passionate
Shepherd to His Love'* (see page 114)*.*

NOVEL

from Captain Corelli's Mandolin

LOUIS DE BERNIÈRES

Love is a temporary madness,
it erupts like volcanoes and then subsides.
And when it subsides you have to make a decision.
You have to work out whether your roots have
so entwined together that it is inconceivable
that you should ever part.
Because this is what love is.
Love is not breathlessness,
it is not excitement,
it is not the promulgation of eternal passion.
That is just being 'in love' which any fool can do.

Love itself is what is left over when being in love
has burned away,
and this is both an art and a fortunate accident.
Those that truly love, have roots that grow
towards each other underground,
and when all the pretty blossom have
fallen from their branches,
they find that they are one tree and not two.

Louis de Bernières (b. 1954) was born in London and spent his earliest years in the Middle East. Captain Corelli's Mandolin *was his fourth novel, published in 1994 and it won 'best book' in the Commonwealth Writers' Prize.*

'Hope' is the Thing with Feathers

EMILY DICKINSON

'Hope' is the thing with feathers –
That perches in the soul –
And sings the tune without the words –
And never stops – at all –

And sweetest – in the Gale – is heard –
And sore must be the storm –
That could abash the little Bird –
That kept so many warm –

I've heard it in the chillest land –
And on the strangest Sea –
Yet, never, in Extremity,
It asked a crumb – of Me.

Emily Dickinson (1830–1886) is considered one of the most original of 19th-century American poets, noted for her unconventional broken rhyming metre and use of dashes and random capitalisation. Most of Dickinson's work remained unknown until after her death.

POEM

Wild Nights

EMILY DICKINSON

Wild Nights – Wild Nights!
Were I with thee
Wild Nights should be
Our luxury!

Futile – the Winds –
To a Heart in port –
Done with the Compass –
Done with the Chart!

Rowing in Eden –
Ah, the Sea!
Might I but moor – Tonight –
In Thee!

The Good-Morrow

POEM

JOHN DONNE

I wonder, by my troth, what thou and I
Did, till we loved; were we not weaned till then,
But sucked on country pleasures, childishly?
Or snorted we in the Seven Sleepers' den?
'Twas so; but this, all pleasures fancies be.
If ever any beauty I did see,
Which I desired, and got, 'twas but a dream of thee.

And now good-morrow to our waking souls,
Which watch not one another out of fear;
For love, all love of other sights controls,
And makes one little room, an everywhere.
Let sea-discoverers to new worlds have gone,
Let maps to others, worlds on worlds have shown,
Let us possess one world; each hath one, and is one.

My face in thine eye, thine in mine appears,
And true plain hearts do in the faces rest;
Where can we find two better hemispheres,
Without sharp North, without declining West?
Whatever dies, was not mixed equally;
If our two loves be one; or thou and I
Love so alike that none do slacken, none can die.

John Donne (1572—1631) was a Protestant reformer in the court of English king James I (James VI of Scotland) and was appointed Dean of St. Paul's Cathedral in 1621. His poetry addressed the nature of human existence and Christian beliefs.

The Anniversary

JOHN DONNE

All Kings, and all their favourites,
    All glory of honours, beauties, wits,
The sun it self, which makes time, as they pass,
Is elder by a year now than it was
When thou and I first one another saw.
All other things to their destruction draw,
    Only our love hath no decay;
This, no tomorrow hath, nor yesterday;
Running it never runs from us away,
But truly keeps his first, last, everlasting day.

Two graves must hide thine and my corse;
    If one might, death were no divorce.
Alas! as well as other princes, we
– Who prince enough in one another be –
Must leave at last in death these eyes and ears,
Oft fed with true oaths, and with sweet salt tears;
    But souls where nothing dwells but love
– All other thoughts being inmates – then shall prove
This or a loved increased there above,
When bodies to their graves, souls from their graves remove.

And then we shall be thoroughly blest;
    But now no more than all the rest.
Here upon earth we're kings, and none but we
Can be such kings, nor of such subjects be.
Who is so safe as we? Where none can do
Treason to us, except one of us two.
    True and false fears let us refrain,
Let us love nobly, and live, and add again
Years and years unto years, till we attain
To write threescore; this is the second of our reign.

For Everything there is a Season

BIBLICAL

ECCLESIASTES 3:1-8

1 There is a time for everything, and a season for every activity under heaven:

2 a time to be born and a time to die, a time to plant and a time to uproot,

3 a time to kill and a time to heal, a time to tear down and a time to build,

4 a time to weep and a time to laugh, a time to mourn and a time to dance,

5 a time to scatter stones and a time to gather them, a time to embrace and a time to refrain,

6 a time to search and a time to give up, a time to keep and a time to throw away,

7 a time to tear and a time to mend, a time to be silent and a time to speak,

8 a time to love and time to hate, a time for war and a time for peace.

New International Version

Two are Better than One

ECCLESIASTES 4:9–12

9   Two are better than one, because they have a good return for
    their work:
10 If one falls down, his friend can help him up. But pity the man
    who falls and has no one to help him up!
11 Also, if two lie down together, they will keep warm. But how
    can one keep warm alone?
12 Though one may be overpowered, two can defend themselves.
    A cord of three strands is not quickly broken.

New International Version

Desiderata

MAX EHRMANN

Go placidly amid the noise and haste, and remember
what peace there may be in silence. As far as
possible without surrender be on good terms with
all persons. Speak your truth quietly and clearly;
and listen to others, even the dull and the ignorant;
they too have their story.

Avoid loud and aggressive persons, they are
vexations to the spirit. If you compare yourself
with others, you may become vain and bitter;
for there will always be greater and lesser persons
than yourself. Enjoy your achievements as well
as your plans.

Keep interested in your own career, however humble;
it is a real possession in the changing fortunes of time.
Exercise caution in your business affairs; for the world
is full of trickery. But let this not blind you to what
virtue there is; many persons strive for high ideals;
and everywhere life is full of heroism.

Be yourself. Especially, do not feign affection.
Neither be cynical about love; for in the face of
all aridity and disenchantment it is as perennial
as the grass.

Take kindly the counsel of the years, gracefully
surrendering the things of youth. Nurture strength
of spirit to shield you in sudden misfortune. But do
not distress yourself with imaginings. Many fears are
born of fatigue and loneliness. Beyond a wholesome
discipline, be gentle with yourself.

You are a child of the universe, no less than the trees
and the stars; you have a right to be here. And whether
or not it is clear to you, no doubt the universe is
unfolding as it should.

Therefore be at peace with God, whatever you conceive
Him to be, and whatever your labours and aspirations,
in the noisy confusion of life keep peace with your
soul. With all its sham, drudgery and broken dreams,
it is still a beautiful world. Be careful. Strive to be happy.

*Max Ehrmann (1872–1945) was an American lawyer and poet. He found
his greatest fame with this prose poem, written in 1927, although the poem did not
become famous until the 1960s. The title is Latin and means, 'things to be desired'.*

A Dedication to my Wife

POEM

T.S. ELIOT

To whom I owe the leaping delight
That quickens my senses in our walkingtime
And the rhythm that governs the repose of our sleepingtime,
The breathing in unison

Of lovers whose bodies smell of each other
Who think the same thoughts without need of speech
And babble the same speech without need of meaning.

No peevish winter wind shall chill
No sullen tropic sun shall wither
The roses in the rose-garden which is ours and ours only

But this dedication is for others to read:
These are my private words addressed to you in public.

83

T. S. Eliot (1888–1965) was a central figure of the modernist movement. This poem celebrates his happy second marriage in 1957 to Valerie Fletcher, his secretary at Faber & Faber.

READING

from Adam Bede

GEORGE ELIOT

What greater thing is there for two human souls
than to feel that they are joined together
to strengthen each other in all labour,
to minister to each other in all sorrow,
to share with each other in all gladness,
to be one with each other in the
silent unspoken memories.

George Eliot (1819–1880) stands amongst the greatest in the canon of English literature. Born Mary Ann Evans, she moved to London where she met Henry Lewes, a married man, with whom, controversially, she lived until his death. Adam Bede *was her first novel, published in 1859.*

from Two Lovers

POEM

GEORGE ELIOT

Two lovers by a moss-grown spring:
They leaned soft cheeks together there,
Mingled the dark and sunny hair,
And heard the wooing thrushes sing.
O budding time! O love's blest prime!

Two wedded from the portal stept:
The bells made happy carolings,
The air was soft as fanning wings,
White petals on the pathway slept.
O pure-eyed bride! O tender pride!

Two faces o'er a cradle bent:
Two hands above the head were locked:
These pressed each other while they rocked,
Those watched a life that love had sent.
O solemn hour! O hidden power!

Two parents by the evening fire:
The red light fell about their knees
On heads that rose by slow degrees
Like buds upon the lily spire.
O patient life! O tender strife!

The red light shone upon the floor
And made the space between them wide;
They drew their chairs up side by side,
Their pale cheeks joined, and said, 'Once more!'
O memories! O past that is!

Blessing For A Marriage

JAMES DILLET FREEMAN

May your marriage bring you all the exquisite excitements a marriage should bring, and may life grant you also patience, tolerance, and understanding.

May you always need one another – not so much to fill your emptiness as to help you to know your fullness. A mountain needs a valley to be complete; the valley does not make the mountain less, but more; and the valley is more a valley because it has a mountain towering over it. So let it be with you and you.

May you need one another, but not out of weakness.
May you want one another, but not out of lack.
May you entice one another, but not compel one another.
May you embrace one another, but not out encircle one another.
May you succeed in all important ways with one another, and not fail in the little graces.
May you look for things to praise, often say, 'I love you!' and take no notice of small faults.

If you have quarrels that push you apart, may both of you hope to have good sense enough to take the first step back.

May you enter into the mystery which is the awareness of one another's presence – no more physical than spiritual, warm and near when you are side by side, and warm and near when you are in separate rooms or even distant cities.
May you have happiness, and may you find it making one another happy.
May you have love, and may you find it loving one another!

James Dillet Freeman (1912–2003) was a central figure in the Christian movement, Unity, as well as a teacher, writer and speaker.

from The Master Speed

POEM

ROBERT FROST

Two such as you with such a master speed
Cannot be parted nor be swept away
From one another once you are agreed
That life is only life forevermore
Together wing to wing and oar to oar.

Robert Frost (1874–1963) is beloved for his choice of rural subjects and use of traditional verse form, which is often belied by a powerful, even dark vision. He is recognised as a central figure in the American poetic canon and he read his poem, 'The Gift Outright' at the inauguration of U.S. President John F. Kennedy.

BIBLICAL

Male and Female, He created them

GENESIS 1:26–28

26 Then God said, 'Let us make man in our image, in our likeness, and let them rule over the fish of the sea and the birds of the air, over the livestock, over all the earth, and over all the creatures that move along the ground.'
27 So God created man in his own image, in the image of God He created him; male and female He created them.
28 God blessed them and said to them, 'Be fruitful and increase in number; fill the earth and subdue it. Rule over the fish of the sea and the birds of the air and over every living creature that moves on the ground.'

New International Version

Creation of Woman

GENESIS 2:20–24

20 So the man gave names to all the livestock, the birds of the air and all the beasts of the field. But for Adam no suitable helper was found.

21 So the LORD God caused the man to fall into a deep sleep; and while he was sleeping, he took one of the man's ribs and closed up the place with flesh.

22 Then the LORD God made a woman from the rib he had taken out of the man, and he brought her to the man.

23 The man said, 'This is now bone of my bones and flesh of my flesh; she shall be called "woman", for she was taken out of man.'

24 For this reason a man will leave his father and mother and be united to his wife, and they will become one flesh.

New International Version

SPIRITUAL

On Children, from The Prophet

KAHLIL GIBRAN

And a woman who held a babe against her bosom said, Speak
to us of Children.
And he said:
Your children are not your children.
They are the sons and daughters of Life's longing for itself.
They come through you but not from you,
And though they are with you yet they belong not to you.

You may give them your love but not your thoughts,
For they have their own thoughts.
You may house their bodies but not their souls,
For their souls dwell in the house of tomorrow, which you
cannot visit, not even in your dreams.
You may strive to be like them, but seek not to make them
like you.
For life goes not backward nor tarries with yesterday.
You are the bows from which your children as living arrows
are sent forth.
The archer sees the mark upon the path of the infinite, and
He bends you with His might that His arrows may go swift
and far.
Let your bending in the archer's hand be for gladness;
For even as He loves the arrow that flies, so He loves also
the bow that is stable.

*Kahlil Gibran (1883–1931) was a Lebanese mystical writer, poet and artist
renowned for his timeless wisdom. He is seen as having a particular affinity with
William Blake. Gibran's* The Prophet, *is his most celebrated statement about the
truths of human experience.*

On Friendship, from The Prophet

KAHLIL GIBRAN

And a youth said, Speak to us of Friendship.
And he answered, saying:
Your friend is your needs answered. He is your field which you
sow with love and reap with thanksgiving. And he is your board
and your fireside. For you come to him with your hunger, and
you seek him for peace.

When your friend speaks his mind you fear not the 'nay' in your
own mind, nor do you withhold the 'ay'. And when he is silent
your heart ceases not to listen to his heart; For without words,
in friendship, all thoughts, all desires, all expectations are born
and shared, with joy that is unclaimed.

When you are part from your friend, you grieve not; For that
which you love most in him may be clearer in his absence, as
the mountain to the climber is clearer from the plain.

And let there be no purpose in friendship save the deepening of
the spirit. For love that seeks aught but the disclosure of its own
mystery is not love but a net cast forth: and only the unprofitable
is caught.

And let your best be for your friend. If he must know the ebb
of your tide, let him know its flood also. For what is your friend
that you should seek him with hours to kill? Seek him always
with hours to live. For it is his to fill your need, but not your
emptiness. And in the sweetness of friendship let there be
laughter, and sharing of pleasures. For in the dew of little things
the heart finds its morning and is refreshed.

SPIRITUAL

On Love, from The Prophet

KAHLIL GIBRAN

Then said Almitra, Speak to us of Love.
And he raised his head and looked upon the people, and there
fell a stillness upon them. And with a great voice he said:
When love beckons to you, follow him,
Though his ways are hard and steep.
And when his wings enfold you yield to him,
Though the sword hidden among his pinions may wound you.
And when he speaks to you believe in him,
Though his voice may shatter your dreams as the north wind
lays waste the garden.

For even as love crowns you so shall he crucify you. Even as he
is for your growth so is he for your pruning.
Even as he ascends to your height and caresses your tenderest
branches that quiver in the sun,
So shall he descend to your roots and shake them in their
clinging to the earth.
Like sheaves of corn he gathers you unto himself.
He threshes you to make you naked.
He sifts you to free you from your husks.
He grinds you to whiteness.
He kneads you until you are pliant;
And then he assigns you to his sacred fire, that you may become
sacred bread for God's sacred feast.

All these things shall love do unto you that you may know the
secrets of your heart, and in that knowledge become a fragment
of Life's heart.

But if in your fear you would seek only love's peace and
love's pleasure,
Then it is better for you that you cover your nakedness and pass
out of love's threshing-floor,
Into the seasonless world where you shall laugh, but not all of
your laughter, and weep, but not all of your tears.
Love gives naught but itself and takes naught but from itself.
Love possesses not nor would it be possessed;
For love is sufficient unto love.

When you love you should not say, 'God is in my heart,' but
rather, 'I am in the heart of God.'
And think not you can direct the course of love, for love, if it
finds you worthy, directs your course.
Love has no other desire but to fulfil itself.
But if you love and must needs have desires, let these be
your desires:
To melt and be like a running brook that sings its melody to
the night.
To know the pain of too much tenderness.
To be wounded by your own understanding of love;
And to bleed willingly and joyfully.
To wake at dawn with a winged heart and give thanks for another
day of loving;
To rest at the noon hour and meditate love's ecstasy;
To return home at eventide with gratitude;
And then to sleep with a prayer for the beloved in your heart and
a song of praise upon your lips.

SPIRITUAL

On Marriage, from The Prophet

KAHLIL GIBRAN

Then Almitra spoke again and said, And what of Marriage,
master?
And he answered saying:
You were born together, and together you shall be forevermore.
You shall be together when the white wings of death scatter
your days.
Ay, you shall be together even in the silent memory of God.
But let there be spaces in your togetherness,
And let the winds of the heavens dance between you.

Love one another, but make not a bond of love:
Let it rather be a moving sea between the shores of your souls.
Fill each other's cup but drink not from one cup.
Give one another of your bread but eat not from the same loaf.
Sing and dance together and be joyous, but let each one of you
be alone,
Even as the strings of a lute are alone though they quiver with
the same music.

Give your hearts, but not into each other's keeping.
For only the hand of Life can contain your hearts.
And stand together yet not too near together:
For the pillars of the temple stand apart,
And the oak tree and the cypress grow not in each other's shadow.

from Far From the Madding Crowd

NOVEL

THOMAS HARDY

He accompanied her up the hill, explaining to her
the details of his forthcoming tenure of the other farm.
They spoke very little of their mutual feeling; pretty
phrases and warm expressions being probably un-
necessary between such tried friends. Theirs was that
substantial affection which arises (if any arises at all)
when the two who are thrown together begin first by
knowing the rougher sides of each other's character,
and not the best till further on, the romance growing
up in the interstices of a mass of hard prosaic reality.
This good-fellowship – CAMARADERIE – usually
occurring through similarity of pursuits, is unfortunately
seldom superadded to love between the sexes, because
men and women associate, not in their labours, but in their
pleasures merely. Where, however, happy circumstance
permits its development, the compounded feeling proves
itself to be the only love which is strong as death -- that
love which many waters cannot quench, nor the floods
drown, beside which the passion usually called by the
name is evanescent as steam.

*Thomas Hardy (1820–1871) is one of Britain's best-loved novelists. He is
renowned for his tragic novels set in Wessex, a fictional county based on his
homeland, the rural West Country.* Far from the Madding Crowd *was Hardy's
fourth novel and first major literary success.*

SONG

My Funny Valentine

LORENZ HART

My funny Valentine, sweet comic Valentine,
You make me smile with my heart.
Your looks are laughable, unphotographable.
Yet, you're my favourite work of art.
Is your figure less than Greek?
Is your mouth a little weak?
When you open it to speak, are you smart?
But don't change a hair for me, not if you care for me.
Stay little Valentine, stay!
Each day is Valentine's day.
Is your figure less than Greek?
Is your mouth a little weak?
When you open it to speak, are you smart?
But please, don't change a hair for me, not if you care for me.
Stay little Valentine, stay!
Each day is Valentine's day.

Lorenz Hart (1895–1943) collaborated on 28 Broadway musicals, writing lyrics for classic songs such as 'The Lady is a Tramp'. 'My Funny Valentine' is a song from the musical Babes in Arms *by Lorenz Hart and Richard Rogers. It has been performed by many great singers, including Ella Fitzgerald and Frank Sinatra.*

from A Farewell to Arms

NOVEL

ERNEST HEMINGWAY

That night ... feeling that we had come home,
feeling no longer alone, waking in the night to
find the other one there, and not gone away; all
other things were unreal. We slept when we were
tired and if we woke the other one woke too so one
was not alone. Often a man wishes to be alone and
a girl wishes to be alone too and if they love each
other they are jealous of that in each other, but I
can truly say we never felt that. We could feel
alone when we were together, alone against the
others ... we were never lonely and never afraid
when we were together.

*Ernest Hemingway (1899–1961) was a part of a set of modernist emigrant
artists that included F. Scott Fitzgerald, James Joyce and Ezra Pound.* A Farewell
to Arms *is a semi-autobiographical novel based on Hemmingway's experiences
in the ambulance service in Italy during the Second World War (1939–1945).*

POEM

Love(III)

GEORGE HERBERT

Love bade me welcome: yet my soul drew back,
Guilty of dust and sin.
But quick-ey'd Love, observing me grow slack
From my first entrance in,
Drew nearer to me, sweetly questioning
If I lack'd any thing.

A guest, I answer'd, worthy to be here:
Love said, You shall be he.
I, the unkind, ungrateful? Ah my dear,
I cannot look on thee.
Love took my hand and smiling did reply,
Who made the eyes but I?

Truth, Lord, but I have marr'd them: let my shame
Go where it doth deserve.
And know you not, says Love, who bore the blame?
My dear, then I will serve.
You must sit down, says Love, and taste my meat:
So I did sit and eat.

George Herbert (1593–1633) was a metaphysical poet and a clergyman. His poems celebrate the many ways of God's love as he discovered them and yet, despite their religious subject, Herbert's quiet intensity and examination of human existence mean they are relevant to the most secular of readers.

The Seven Steps

HINDU MARRIAGE POEM

We have taken the seven steps
You have become mine forever.
Yes, we have become partners.
I have become yours.
Hereafter, I cannot live without you.
Do not live without me.
Let us share the joys.
We are word and meaning, united.
You are thought and I am sound.

May the night be honey-sweet for us;
May the morning be honey-sweet for us;
May the earth be honey-sweet for us
And the heavens be honey-sweet for us.
May the plants be honey-sweet for us;
May the sun be all honey for us;
May the cows yield us honey-sweet milk.
As the heavens are stable,
As the earth is stable,
As the mountains are stable,
As the whole universe is stable,
So may our unions be perfectly settled.

*This is a modern interperpretation of the words stated as part of the Hindu
wedding vows. It incorporates phrasings from the ritual of the Seven Steps when
the bride's sari is tied to the groom's kurta and he leads her in seven steps around
a fire whilst the priest chants seven blessings for a strong marriage.*

POEM

At the Wedding-March

GERARD MANLEY HOPKINS

God with honour hang your head,
Groom, and grace you, bride, your bed
With lissome scions, sweet scions,
Out of hallowed bodies bred.

Each be other's comfort kind:
Déep, déeper than divined,
Divine charity, dear charity,
Fast you ever, fast bind.

Then let the March tread our ears:
I to him turn with tears
Who to wedlock, his wonder wedlock,
Déals tríumph and immortal years.

Gerard Manley Hopkins (1844–1889) was a priest and a poet. During the year of his ordination he wrote 11 extraordinary sonnets that expressed his Christian faith. His poems, first published in 1918, were instantly hailed as experimental and modern and have since inspired many 20th-century poets.

Lovesong

POEM

TED HUGHES

He loved her and she loved him.
His kisses sucked out her whole past and future or tried to
He had no other appetite
She bit him she gnawed him she sucked
She wanted him complete inside her
Safe and sure forever and ever
Their little cries fluttered into the curtains

Her eyes wanted nothing to get away
Her looks nailed down his hands his wrists his elbows
He gripped her hard so that life
Should not drag her from that moment
He wanted all future to cease
He wanted to topple with his arms round her
Off that moment's brink and into nothing
Or everlasting or whatever there was

Her embrace was an immense press
To print him into her bones
His smiles were the garrets of a fairy palace
Where the real world would never come
Her smiles were spider bites
So he would lie still till she felt hungry
His words were occupying armies
Her laughs were an assassin's attempts
His looks were bullets daggers of revenge
His glances were ghosts in the corner with horrible secrets

His whispers were whips and jackboots
Her kisses were lawyers steadily writing
His caresses were the last hooks of a castaway
Her love-tricks were the grinding of locks
And their deep cries crawled over the floors
Like an animal dragging a great trap
His promises were the surgeon's gag
Her promises took the top off his skull
She would get a brooch made of it
His vows pulled out all her sinews
He showed her how to make a love-knot
Her vows put his eyes in formalin
At the back of her secret drawer
Their screams stuck in the wall

Their heads fell apart into sleep like the two halves
Of a lopped melon, but love is hard to stop

In their entwined sleep they exchanged arms and legs
In their dreams their brains took each other hostage

In the morning they wore each other's face

Ted Hughes (1930–1998) was Poet Laureate from 1984. Married to the poet Sylvia Plath, he is known for his almost primitive poetry that often focuses on the natural world. In 'Lovesong', he depicts love as something both brutally physical yet somehow also beautiful in its intimacy.

from Les Miserables

VICTOR HUGO

You can give without loving, but you can never
love without giving. The great acts of love are
done by those who are habitually performing
small acts of kindness. We pardon to the extent
that we love. Love is knowing that even when you
are alone, you will never be lonely again. And
great happiness of life is the conviction that we
are loved. Loved for ourselves. And even loved
in spite of ourselves.

Victor Hugo (1802–1885) is best known for his novel Les Miserables, *a
panoramic piece of social history written while he was in exile in Guernsey due to
his republican beliefs. Although Hugo was frequently punished for his political
views, he was made a senator in 1876 and buried a national hero in the Panthéon.*

READING

from Yi Jing, I Ching, The Classic of Changes

I CHING

... When two people are at one
in their inmost hearts,
they shatter even the strength of iron or bronze.
And when two people understand each other
in their inmost hearts,
their words are sweet and strong,
like the fragrance of orchids.

I Ching, meaning 'Classic of Changes', is one of the oldest of the Chinese classics, possibly dating back to about 2800 BC. It is a system of divination and resembles cosmology and philosophy central to Chinese cultural beliefs.

Song: To Celia

POEM

BEN JONSON

Drink to me, only with thine eyes
And I will pledge with mine;
Or leave a kiss but in the cup,
And I'll not look for wine.
The thirst that from the soul doth rise
Doth ask a drink divine:
But might I of Jove's nectar sup
I would not change for thine.

I sent thee late a rosy wreath,
Not so much honouring thee
As giving it a hope that there
It could not withered be
But thou thereon didst only breathe
And sent'st it back to me:
Since, when it grows and smells, I swear,
Not of itself but thee.

Ben Jonson (1572–1637) was a leading Jacobean playwright, known for his satirical and witty comedies such as Volpone. *He was part of a group of writers who gathered at the Mermaid tavern in Cheapside, London, where he had a great influence on younger poets and writers. This poem was written in 1616.*

POEM

Bright Star,
Would I Were Steadfast as Thou Art

JOHN KEATS

Bright star, would I were steadfast as thou art —
Not in lone splendour hung aloft the night,
And watching, with eternal lids apart,
Like nature's patient sleepless eremite,
The moving waters at their priestlike task
Of pure ablution round earth's human shores,
Or gazing on the new soft-fallen mask
Of snow upon the mountains and the moors;
No — yet still steadfast, still unchangeable,
Pillow'd upon my fair love's ripening breast,
To feel for ever its soft fall and swell,
Awake for ever in a sweet unrest,
Still, still to hear her tender-taken breath,
And so live ever — or else swoon to death.

*John Keats (1795—1821) was a leading figure in the Romantic Movement.
His poetry displays a wealth of sensuous imagery, inspired by the emotions
aroused by the natural world. He died of consumption in Rome, aged 26. Despite
the brevity of his life, Keats' poems created a landmark in English poetry.*

Married Love

READING

KUAN TAO-SHENG

You and I have so much love
That it burns like a fire,
In which we bake a lump of clay
Moulded into a figure of you
And a figure of me.
Then we take both of them,
And break them into pieces,
And mix the pieces with water,
And mould again a figure of you,
And a figure of me.
I am in your clay.
You are in my clay.
In life we share a single quilt,
In death we will share one bed.

Kuan Tao-sheng (1263–1319) was the wife of the renowned Chinese scholar and artist, Chao Meng-Fu. She is a prominent figure in the history of bamboo painting and is one of the few women who is mentioned in early Western surveys of Chinese painting.

POEM

Let my Shadow Disappear into Yours

PAR LAGERKVIST

Let my shadow disappear into yours.
Let me lose myself
under the tall trees,
that themselves lose their crowns in the twilight,
surrendering themselves to the sky and the night.

Par Lagerkvist (1891–1974) decided early in life that he was going to be a writer and, after a year at the University of Uppsala, he left for Paris where he came under the influence of expressionism. He won the Nobel Prize for literature in 1951.

Wedding-wind

POEM

PHILIP LARKIN

The wind blew all my wedding-day,
And my wedding-night was the night of the high wind;
And a stable door was banging, again and again,
That he must go and shut it, leaving me
Stupid in candlelight, hearing rain,
Seeing my face in the twisted candlestick,
Yet seeing nothing. When he came back
He said the horses were restless, and I was sad
That any man or beast that night should lack
The happiness I had.

Now in the day
All's ravelled under the sun by the wind's blowing.
He has gone to look at the floods, and I
Carry a chipped pail to the chicken-run,
Set it down, and stare. All is the wind
Hunting through clouds and forests, thrashing
My apron and the hanging cloths on the line.
Can it be borne, this bodying-forth by wind
Of joy my actions turn on, like a thread
Carrying beads? Shall I be let to sleep
Now this perpetual morning shares my bed?
Can even death dry up
These new delighted lakes, conclude
Our kneeling as cattle by the all-generous waters.

*Philip Larkin (1922–1985) was a poet, novelist, librarian and jazz critic.
In his poetry he merges the colloquialism and slang of the day with traditional and
even archaic forms. Larkin captures the essence of post-war Britain with his use of
the tones and rhythms of daily life in suburban England.*

POEM

from Fidelity

D.H. LAWRENCE

Man and woman are like the earth, that brings forth flowers
in summer, and love, but underneath is rock.
Older than flowers, older than ferns, older than foraminiferae,
older than plasm altogether is the soul underneath.

And when, throughout all the wild orgasms of love
slowly a gem forms, in the ancient, once-more-molten rocks
of two human hearts, two ancient rocks,
a man's heart and a woman's,
that is the crystal of peace, the slow hard jewel of trust,
the sapphire of fidelity.
The gem of mutual peace emerging from the wild chaos of love.

*D.H. Lawrence (1885–1930) was an English novelist and poet, most
famous for his novels, including* The Rainbow *and* Lady Chatterley's Lover. *His
writing is almost always concerned with human emotions and consciousness and
has, in turn, provoked both sharp criticism and deep respect.*

The Owl and the Pussy-Cat

EDWARD LEAR

The Owl and the Pussy-Cat went to sea
In a beautiful pea-green boat,
They took some honey, and plenty of money
Wrapped up in a five–pound note
The Owl looked up to the stars above
And sang to a small guitar
'O lovely Pussy! O Pussy, my love,
What a beautiful Pussy you are,
    You are
    You are!
What a beautiful Pussy you are!'

Pussy said to the Owl 'You elegant fowl!
How charmingly sweet you sing!
O let us be married! Too long we have tarried
But what shall we do for a ring?'
They sailed away, for a year and a day
To the land where the Bong-tree grows
And there in a wood a Piggy-wig stood
With a ring at the end of his nose
    His nose
    His nose!
With a ring at the end of his nose.

'Dear Pig, are you willing to sell for one shilling
Your ring?' Said the Piggy, 'I will.'
So they took it away and were married next day
By the turkey who lives on the hill.

They dined on mince, and slices of quince
Which they ate with a runcible spoon
And hand in hand, on the edge of the sand
They danced by the light of the moon
    The moon!
    The moon!
They danced by the light of the moon.

Edward Lear (1812–1888) is primarily remembered for his nonsense poetry, his use of invented words and the fantastical sketches with which he illustrated his poems. His favourite form was the limerick, which he popularised. He is believed to have written this poem for Janet Symonds, the young daughter of a friend.

The Newly-wedded

POEM

WINTHROP MACKWORTH PRAED

Now the rite is duly done;
Now the word is spoken;
And the spell has made us one
Which may ne'er be broken:
Rest we, dearest, in our home, -
Roam we o'er the heather, -
We shall rest, and we shall roam,
Shall we not? together.

From this hour the summer rose
Sweeter breathes to charm us;
From this hour the winter snows
Lighter fall to harm us:
Fair or foul – on land or sea –
Come the wind or weather,
Best and worst, whate'er they be,
We shall share together.

Death, who friend from friend can part,
Brother rend from brother,
Shall but link us, heart and heart,
Closer to each other:
We will call his anger play,
Deem his dart a feather,
When we meet him on our way
Hand in hand together.

Winthrop Mackworth Praed (1802–1839) was educated at Eton College and Cambridge University. He became a lawyer and a politician, but also wrote poetry. His poems are known for their style, rhythm and wit.

POEM

The Passionate Shepherd to His Love

CHRISTOPHER MARLOWE

Come live with me, and be my Love,
And we will all the pleasures prove,
That valleys, groves, hills and fields,
Woods, or steepy mountain yields.

And we will sit upon the rocks,
Seeing the shepherds feed their flocks
By shallow rivers, to whose falls
Melodious birds sing madrigals.

And I will make thee beds of roses,
And a thousand fragrant posies,
A cap of flowers, and a kirtle,
Embroidered all with leaves of myrtle.

A gown made of the finest wool
Which from our pretty lambs we pull,
Fair-lined slippers for the cold,
With buckles of the purest gold.

A belt of straw and ivy buds,
With coral clasps and amber studs,
And if these pleasures may thee move,
Come live with me, and be my Love.

The shepherds' swains shall dance and sing
For thy delight each May-morning;
If these delights thy mind may move,
Then live with me, and be my Love.

*Christopher Marlowe (1564–1593) was one of the first dramatists to use
blank verse to its full effect; his tragedies were a forerunner of William
Shakespeare's and he is thought to have contributed to some of Shakespeare's
work. This poem inspired C. Day Lewis' poem 'Song' (see page 73).*

To His Coy Mistress

POEM

A N D R E W   M A R V E L L

Had we but world enough, and time.
This coyness, lady, were no crime.
We would sit down, and think which way
To walk, and pass our long love's day.
Thou by the Indian Ganges' side
Should'st rubies find: I by the tide
Of Humber would complain. I would
Love you ten years before the Flood,
And you should, if you please, refuse
Till the conversion of the Jews.
My vegetable love should grow
Vaster than empires, and more slow
An hundred years should go to praise
Thine eyes, and on thy forehead gaze;
Two hundred to adore each breast;
But thirty thousand to the rest;
An age at least to every part,
And the last age should show your heart.
For lady, you deserve this state,
Nor would I love at lower rate.

But at my back I always hear
Time's winged chariot hurrying near:
And yonder all before us lie
Deserts of vast eternity.
Thy beauty shall no more be found;
Nor, in thy marble vault, shall sound
My echoing song: then worms shall try

115

That long-preserved virginity,
And your quaint honour turn to dust,
And into ashes all my lust.
The grave's a fine and private place,
But none, I think, do there embrace.

Now, therefore, while the youthful hue
Sits on thy skin like morning dew,
And while thy willing soul transpires
At every pore with instant fires,
Now let us sport us while we may;
And now, like amorous birds of prey,
Rather at once our Time devour,
Than languish in his slow-chapt power.
Let us roll all our strength and all
Our sweetness up into one ball,
And tear our pleasures with rough strife
Through the iron gates of life.
Thus, though we cannot make our Sun
Stand still, yet we will make him run.

Andrew Marvell (1621–1678) was a metaphysical poet admired for his sensuous and witty verse. His poetry echoes John Donne and the metaphysical school. He was also influenced by Ben Johnson and John Milton.

The Beatitudes

MATTHEW 5:1–10

1 Now when he saw the crowds, he went up on a mountainside and sat down. His disciples came to him,
2 and he began to teach them, saying:
3 'Blessed are the poor in spirit, for theirs is the kingdom of heaven.
4 Blessed are those who mourn, for they will be comforted.
5 Blessed are the meek, for they will inherit the earth.
6 Blessed are those who hunger and thirst for righteousness, for they will be filled.
7 Blessed are the merciful, for they will be shown mercy.
8 Blessed are the pure in heart, for they will see God.
9 Blessed are the peacemakers, for they will be called sons of God.
10 Blessed are those who are persecuted because of righteousness, for theirs is the kingdom of heaven.'

New International Version

POEM

Believe me,
if All those Endearing Young Charms

THOMAS MOORE

Believe me, if all those endearing young charms,
Which I gaze on so fondly to-day
Were to change by to-morrow, and fleet in my arms,
Like fairy-gifts fading away,
Thou wouldst still be adored, as this moment thou art,
Let thy loveliness fade as it will,
And around the dear ruin each wish of my heart
Would entwine itself verdantly still.

It is not while beauty and youth are thine own,
And thy cheeks unprofaned by a tear,
That the fervor and faith of a soul can be known,
To which time will but make thee more dear;
No, the heart that has truly loved never forgets,
But as truly loves on to the close,
As the sun-flower turns on her god, when he sets,
The same look which she turned when he rose.

Thomas Moore (1779–1852) was born into a Roman Catholic family in Ireland at the height of Catholic oppression. He enjoyed literary success akin to that of his contemporaries, Lord Byron and Shelley, and the Irish Ordinance Board tried to establish an Irish Poet Laureate specifically to honour him.

from Love is Enough

POEM

WILLIAM MORRIS

Love is enough: though the World be a-waning,
And the woods have no voice but the voice of complaining,
Though the sky be too dark for dim eyes to discover
The gold-cups and daisies fair blooming thereunder,
Though the hills be held shadows, and the sea a dark wonder,
And this day draw a veil over all deeds pass'd over,
Yet their hands shall not tremble, their feet shall not falter;
The void shall not weary, the fear shall not alter
These lips and these eyes of the loved and the lover.

William Morris (1834–1896) was a member of the Pre-Raphaelite brotherhood. In this poem, Morris has attempted to reconstruct the alliterative language of Old English poetry. The poem in its entirety tells of a king who abandons his throne for love of a woman.

NOVEL

from Jazz

TONI MORRISON

It's nice when grown people whisper to each other under the covers. Their ecstasy is more leaf-sigh than bray and the body is the vehicle, not the point. They reach, grown people, for something beyond, way beyond and way, way down underneath tissue. They are remembering while they whisper the carnival dolls they won and the Baltimore boats they never sailed on. The pears they let hang on the limb because if they plucked them, they would be gone from there and who else would see that ripeness if they took it away for themselves? How could anybody passing by see them and imagine for themselves what the flavour would be like? Breathing and murmuring under covers both of them have washed and hung out on the line, in a bed they chose together and kept together nevermind one leg was propped on a 1916 dictionary, and the mattress, curved like a preacher's palm asking for witnesses in His name's sake, enclosed them each and every night and muffled their whispering, old-time love.

They are under the covers because they don't have to look at themselves anymore; there is no stud's eye, no chippie glance to undo them. They are inward toward the other, bound and joined by carnival dolls and the steamers that sailed from ports they never saw. That is what is beneath their undercover whispers.

Toni Morrison (b. 1931) is an editor and academic as well as an author. Her literature explores the African-American experience in many forms and she won the Nobel Prize in Literature in 1993. Jazz is a tale of love and obsession and conjures up the hopes, fears, loves and realities of black urban life in the 1920s.

from A Gift from the Sea

ANNE MORROW LINDBERGH

One recognises the truth of Saint Exupery's line: Love does
not consist in gazing at each other. But in looking outward
together in the same direction. For in fact, man and woman
are not only looking outward in the same direction, they are
working outward. Here one forms ties, roots, a firm base....
Here one makes oneself part of the community of men, of
human society. Here the bonds of marriage are formed. For
marriage, which is always spoken of as a bond, becomes
actually, in this stage, many bonds, many strands, of different
texture and strength, making up a web that is taut and firm.
The web is fashioned of love. Yes, but many kinds of love:
romantic love first, then a slow-growing devotion and, playing
through these, a constantly rippling companionship. It is made
of loyalties, and interdependencies, and shared experiences.
It is woven of memories of meetings and conflicts; of triumphs
and disappointments. It is a web of communication, a common
language, and the acceptance of lack of language too, a
knowledge of likes and dislikes, of habits and reactions, both
physical and mental. It is a web of instincts and intuitions,
and known and unknown exchanges. The web of marriage
is made by propinquity, in the day to day living side by side,
looking outward and working outward in the same direction.
It is woven in space and in time of the substance of life itself.

*Anne Morrow Lindbergh (1906–2001) was a pioneering American
aviator who completed over 40,000 miles of exploratory flying. She wrote* A Gift
from the Sea *in 1955, as a series of meditations – on youth, age, love, marriage,
peace, solitude and contentment – set down during a brief vacation by the sea.*

POEM

Reprise

OGDEN NASH

Geniuses of countless nations
Have told their love for generations
Till all their memorable phrases
Are common as goldenrod or daisies.
Their girls have glimmered like the moon,
Or shimmered like a summer moon,
Stood like a lily, fled like a fawn,
Now the sunset, now the dawn,
Here the princess in the tower
There the sweet forbidden flower.
Darling, when I look at you
Every aged phrase is new,
And there are moments when it seems
I've married one of Shakespeare's dreams.

*Ogden Nash (1902–1971) was one of America's foremost comic poets.
He wrote witty verse for magazines such as the* New Yorker *and is known for his
use of puns, parody, pastiche and alliteration both to amuse and shock.*

Tin Wedding Whistle

OGDEN NASH

Though you know it anyhow
Listen to me, darling, now,
Proving what I need not prove
How I know I love you, love.
Near and far, near and far,
I am happy where you are;
Likewise I have never learnt
How to be it where you aren't.
Far and wide, far and wide,
I can walk with you beside;
Furthermore, I tell you what,
I sit and sulk where you are not.
Visitors remark my frown
When you're upstairs and I am down,
Yes, and I'm afraid I pout
When I'm indoors and you are out;
But how contentedly I view
Any room containing you.
In fact I care not where you be,
Just as long as it's with me.
In all your absences I glimpse
Fire and flood and trolls and imps.
Is your train a minute slothful?
I goad the stationmaster wrothful.

When with friends to bridge you drive
I never know if you're alive,
And when you linger late in shops
I long to telephone the cops.
Yet how worth the waiting for,
To see you coming through the door.
Somehow, I can be complacent
Never but with you adjacent.
Near and far, near and far,
I am happy where you are;
Likewise I have never learnt
How to be it where you aren't.
Then grudge me not my fond endeavour,
To hold you in my sight forever;
Let none, not even you, disparage
Such a valid reason for a marriage.

We Have Lost Even

PABLO NERUDA

We have lost even this twilight.
No one saw us this evening hand in hand
while the blue night dropped on the world.

I have seen from my window
the fiesta of sunset in the distant mountain tops.

Sometimes a piece of sun
burned like a coin in my hand.

I remembered you with my soul clenched
in that sadness of mine that you know.

Where were you then?
Who else was there?
Saying what?
Why will the whole of love come on me suddenly
when I am sad and feel you are far away?

The book fell that always closed at twilight
and my blue sweater rolled like a hurt dog at my feet.

Always, always you recede through the evenings
toward the twilight erasing statues.

Pablo Neruda (1904–1973) was a politically active Chilean poet. His love poetry captured the imagination of the world: his volume Twenty Love Songs and a Song of Despair *has sold over one million copies. Neruda was awarded the Nobel Prize in literature in 1971.*

POEM

Love Sonnet IX

PABLO NERUDA

There where the waves shatter on the restless rocks
the clear light bursts and enacts its rose,
and the sea-circle shrinks to a cluster of buds,
to one drop of blue salt, falling.

O bright magnolia bursting in the foam,
magnetic transient whose death blooms
and vanishes – being, nothingness – forever:
broken salt, dazzling lurch of the sea.

You & I, Love, together we ratify the silence,
while the sea destroys its perpetual statues,
collapses its towers of wild speed and whiteness:

because in the weavings of those invisible fabrics,
galloping water, incessant sand,
we make the only permanent tenderness.

Love Sonnet XLV

PABLO NERUDA

Don't go far off, not even for a day, because –
because – I don't know how to say it: a day is long
and I will be waiting for you, as in an empty station
when the trains are parked off somewhere else, asleep.

Don't leave me, even for an hour, because
then the little drops of anguish will all run together,
the smoke that roams looking for a home will drift
into me, choking my lost heart.

Oh, may your silhouette never dissolve on the beach;
may your eyelids never flutter into the empty distance.
Don't leave me for a second, my dearest,

because in that moment you'll have gone so far
I'll wander mazily over all the earth, asking,
Will you come back? Will you leave me here, dying?

POEM

Love Sonnet XVII

PABLO NERUDA

I don't love you as if you were the salt-rose, topaz
or arrow of carnations that propagate fire:
I love you as certain dark things are loved,
secretly, between the shadow and the soul.

I love you as the plant that doesn't bloom and carries
hidden within itself the light of those flowers,
and thanks to your love, darkly in my body
lives the dense fragrance that rises from the earth.

I love you without knowing how, or when, or from where,
I love you simply, without problems or pride:
I love you in this way because I don't know any other way of loving

but this, in which there is no I or you,
so intimate that your hand upon my chest is my hand,
so intimate that when I fall asleep it is your eyes that close.

Love

PABLO NERUDA

Because of you, in gardens of blossoming flowers I ache from the perfumes of spring.

I have forgotten your face, I no longer remember your hands; how did your lips feel on mine?

Because of you, I love the white statues drowsing in the parks, the white statues that have neither voice nor sight.

I have forgotten your voice, your happy voice; I have forgotten your eyes.

Like a flower to its perfume, I am bound to my vague memory of you. I live with pain that is like a wound; if you touch me, you will do me irreparable harm.

Your caresses enfold me, like climbing vines on melancholy walls.

I have forgotten your love, yet I seem to glimpse you in every window.

Because of you, the heady perfumes of summer pain me; because of you, I again seek out the signs that precipitate desires: shooting
stars, falling objects.

POEM

Morning Love Sonnet XXVII

PABLO NERUDA

Naked, you are simple as a hand,
smooth, earthy, small ... transparent, round.
You have moon lines and apple paths;
Naked, you are slender as the wheat.

Naked, Cuban blue midnight is your colour,
Naked, I trace the stars and vines in your hair;
Naked, you are spacious and yellow
As a summer's wholeness in a golden church.

Naked, you are tiny as your fingernail;
Subtle and curved in the rose-coloured dawn
And you withdraw to the underground world

As if down a long tunnel of clothing and of chores:
your clear light dims, gets dressed, drops its leaves,
And becomes a naked hand again.

Why Marriage?

MARI NICHOLS

Because to the depths of me, I long to love one person,
With all my heart, my soul, my mind, my body...

Because I need a forever friend to trust with the intimacies of me,
Who won't hold them against me,
Who loves me when I'm unlikable,
Who sees the small child in me, and
Who looks for the divine potential of me...

Because I need to cuddle in the warmth of the night
With someone who thanks God for me,
With someone I feel blessed to hold...
Because marriage means opportunity
To grow in love in friendship...

Because marriage is a discipline
To be added to a list of achievements...
Because marriages do not fail, people fail
When they enter into marriage
Expecting another to make them whole...

Because, knowing this,
I promise myself to take full responsibility
For my spiritual, mental and physical wholeness
I create me, I take half of the responsibility for my marriage
Together we create our marriage...

Because with this understanding
The possibilities are limitless.

Marriage Joins Two People in the Circle of its Love

EDMUND O'NEILL

Marriage is a commitment to life, the best that two people can find and bring out in each other. It offers opportunities for sharing and growth that no other relationship can equal. It is a physical and an emotional joining that is promised for a lifetime.

Within the circle of its love, marriage encompasses all of life's most important relationships. A wife and a husband are each other's best friend, confidant, lover, teacher, listener, and critic. And there may come times when one partner is heartbroken or ailing, and the love of the other may resemble the tender caring of a parent for a child.

Marriage deepens and enriches every facet of life. Happiness is fuller, memories are fresher, commitment is stronger, even anger is felt more strongly, and passes away more quickly.

Marriage understands and forgives the mistakes life is unable to avoid. It encourages and nurtures new life, new experiences, and new ways of expressing a love that is deeper than life.

When two people pledge their love and care for each other in marriage, they create a spirit unique unto themselves which binds them closer than any spoken or written words. Marriage is a promise, a potential made in the hearts of two people who love each other and takes a lifetime to fulfil.

A White Rose

POEM

JOHN BOYLE O'REILLY

The red rose whispers of passion,
And the white rose breathes of love;
O the red rose is a falcon,
And the white rose is a dove.

But I send you a cream-white rosebud
With a flush on its petal tips;
For the love that is purest and sweetest
Has a kiss of desire on the lips.

John Boyle O'Reilly (1844–1890) was a journalist and political agitator. Born in Dublin, he reported on the Manchester Guardian, *where he joined the revolutionary movement, the Fenians and returned to Dublin. He was sentenced to 20 years' servitude in Australia for spreading Fenianism and finally settled in Boston.*

POEM

Wedding

ALICE OSWALD

From time to time our love is like a sail
and when the sail begins to alternate
from tack to tack, it's like a swallowtail
and when the swallow flies it's like a coat;
and if the coat is yours, it has a tear
like a wide mouth and when the mouth begins
to draw the wind, it's like a trumpeter
and when the trumpet blows, it blows like millions....
and this, my love, when millions come and go
beyond the need of us, is like a trick;
and when the trick begins, it's like a toe
tip-toeing on a rope, which is like luck;
and when the luck begins, it's like a wedding,
which is like love, which is like everything.

Alice Oswald (b. 1966) works as a gardener and lives in Dartington, Devon. The nature surrounding her is central to her writing: her first collection of poetry reflects her love of gardening and her second, Dart, *tells the story of the river Dart.*

from A Wedding

POEM

BORIS PASTERNAK

Into the enormous sky flew
a whirlwind of blue-gray patches –
a flock of doves spiraling up
suddenly from the dovecotes.

And to see them makes you wish,
just as the wedding-feast is ending,
years of happiness for this couple,
flung onto the wind like doves.

Life too is only an instant,
only a dissolving of ourselves
into everyone,
as if we gave ourselves as gifts.

Only a wedding, only the depths
of a window and the sound rushing in,
only a song, or a dream
only a blue-gray dove.

Boris Pasternak (1890–1960) was a leading Russian intellectual, poet and novelist. He is probably most famous for his celebrated novel Doctor Zhivago.

Never Marry but for Love

WILLIAM PENN

Never marry but for love; but see that thou lovest what is lovely. He that minds a body and not a soul has not the better part of that relationship, and will consequently lack the noblest comfort of a married life.

Between a man and his wife nothing ought to rule but love. As love ought to bring them together, so it is the best way to keep them well together.

A husband and wife that love one another show their children that they should do so too. Others visibly lose their authority in their families by their contempt of one another, and teach their children to be unnatural by their own examples.

Let not enjoyment lessen, but augment, affection; it being the basest of passions to like when we have not, what we slight when we possess.

Here it is we ought to search out our pleasure, where the field is large and full of variety, and of an enduring nature; sickness, poverty or disgrace being not able to shake it because it is not under the moving influences of worldly contingencies.

Nothing can be more entire and without reserve; nothing more zealous, affectionate and sincere; nothing more contented than such a couple, nor greater temporal felicity than to be one of them.

William Penn (1644–1718) is regarded as one of America's first great champions for liberty and peace. During the period of great religious persecution in America in the late 17th century, Penn established a Quaker settlement in America, which became the state of Pennsylvania, which protected freedom of conscience.

The Art of a Good Marriage

WILFERD ARLAN PETERSON

Happiness in marriage is not something that just happens.
A good marriage must be created.
In marriage the little things are the big things.
It is never being too old to hold hands.
It is remembering to say 'I love you' at least once a day.
It is never going to sleep angry.
It is at no time taking the other for granted; the courtship
should not end with the honeymoon, it should continue
through all the years.
It is having a mutual sense of values and common objectives.
It is standing together facing the world.
It is forming a circle of love that gathers in the whole family.
It is doing things for each other, not in the attitude of duty or
sacrifice, but in the spirit of joy.
It is speaking words of appreciation and demonstrating
gratitude in thoughtful ways.
It is not looking for perfection in each other.
It is cultivating flexibility, patience, understanding and a
sense of humour.
It is having the capacity to forgive and forget.
It is giving each other an atmosphere in which each can grow.
It is a common search for the good and the beautiful.
It is establishing a relationship in which the independence is
equal, dependence is mutual and the obligation is reciprocal.
It is not only marrying the right partner, it is being the
right partner.

*Wilferd Arlan Peterson (1900–1995) was married for 58 years and 'The
Art of a Good Marriage' is a touchstone for many couples. It embodies the
sentiments, the ideals and the love to which any marriage aspires.*

from the Symposium

PLATO

Humans have never understood the power of Love, for if
they had they would surely have built noble temples and
altars and offered solemn sacrifices; but this is not done,
and most certainly ought to be done, since Love is our best
friend, our helper, and the healer of the ills which prevent
us from being happy.

To understand the power of Love, we must understand that
our original human nature was not like it is now, but different.
Human beings each had two sets of arms, two sets of legs,
and two faces looking in opposite directions. There were
three sexes then: one comprised of two men called the
children of the Sun, one made of two women called the
children of the Earth, and a third made of a man and a
woman, called the children of the Moon. Due to the power
and might of these original humans, the Gods began to fear
that their reign might be threatened. They sought for a
way to end the humans' insolence without destroying them.

It was at this point that Zeus divided the humans in half.
After the division the two parts of each desiring their other
half, came together, and throwing their arms about one
another, entwined in mutual embraces, longing to grow
into one. So ancient is the desire of one another which is
implanted in us, reuniting our original nature, making one
of two, and healing the state of humankind.

Each of us when separated, having one side only, is but the indenture of a person, and we are always looking for our other half. Those whose original nature lies with the children of the Sun are men who are drawn to other men, those from the children of the Earth are women who love other women, and those from the children of the Moon are men and women drawn to one another. And when one of us meets our other half, we are lost in an amazement of love and friendship and intimacy, and would not be out of the other's sight even for a moment. We pass our whole lives together, desiring that we should be melted into one, to spend our lives as one person instead of two, and so that after our death there will be one departed soul instead of two; this is the very expression of our ancient need. And the reason is that human nature was originally one and we were a whole, and the desire and pursuit of the whole is called Love.

Plato (c. 428–c. 348 BC) was born in Athens and his work established the Academy, a centre of philosophical, mathematical and scientific research. The 'Symposium' is one of the foundational documents of Western culture and arguably the most profound analysis and celebration of love in the history of philosophy.

A Good Wife is More Precious than Jewels

PROVERBS 31:10-12, 25-31

10 A wife of noble character who can find? She is worth far more than rubies.

11 Her husband has full confidence in her and lacks nothing of value.

12 She brings him good, not harm, all the days to come.

25 She is clothed with strength and dignity; she can laugh at the days to come.

26 She speaks with wisdom, and faithful instruction is on her tongue.

27 She watches over the affairs of her household and does not eat the bread of idleness.

28 Her children arise and call her blessed; her husband also, and he praises her:

29 'Many women do noble things, but you surpass them all.'

30 Charm is deceptive, and beauty is fleeting; but a woman who fears the LORD is to be praised.

31 Give her the reward she has earned, and let her works bring her praise at the city gate.

New International Version

May God be Gracious to us and Bless us...

PSALM 67

1 May God be gracious to us and bless us and make his face shine upon us, Selah

2 that your ways may be known on earth, your salvation among all nations.

3 May the peoples praise you, O God; may all the peoples praise you.

4 May the nations be glad and sing for joy, for you rule the peoples justly and guide the nations of the earth. Selah

5 May the peoples praise you, O God; may all the peoples praise you.

6 Then the land will yield its harvest, and God, our God, will bless us.

7 God will bless us, and all the ends of the earth will fear him.

New International Version

Let us Sing to the Lord

PSALM 95:1−7

1 Come, let us sing for joy to the LORD; let us shout aloud
to the Rock of our salvation.
2 Let us come before him with music and song.
3 For the LORD is the great God, the great King above
all gods.
4 In his hand are the depths of the earth, and the mountain
peaks belong to him.
5 The sea is his, for he made it, and his hands formed the
dry land.
6 Come, let us bow down in worship, let us kneel before
the LORD our Maker;
7 for he is our God and we are the people of his pasture, the
flock under his care.

New International Version

Make a Joyful Noise to the Lord

BIBLICAL

PSALM 100

1 Shout for joy to the LORD, all the earth.
2 Worship the LORD with gladness; come before him with joyful songs.
3 Know that the LORD is God. It is he who made us, and we are his; we are his people, the sheep of his pasture.
4 Enter his gates with thanksgiving and his courts with praise; give thanks to him and praise his name.
5 For the LORD is good and his love endures forever; his faithfulness continues through all generations.

143

New International Version

BIBLICAL

He will Keep your Going Out and your Coming In

PSALM 121

1   I lift up my eyes to the hills – where does my help come from?
2   My help comes from the LORD, the Maker of heaven and
    earth.
3   He will not let your foot slip – he who watches over you will
    not slumber;
4   indeeed, he who watches over Israel will neither slumber
    nor sleep.
5   The LORD watches over you – the LORD is your shade at
    your right hand;
6   the sun will not harm you by day, nor the moon by night.
7   The LORD will keep you from all harm – he will watch over
    your life;
8   the LORD will watch over your coming and going both now
    and forevermore.

144

New International Version

May you See your Children's Children

PSALM 128

1 Blessed are all who fear the LORD, who walk in
   his ways.
2 You will eat the fruit of your labour; blessings and
   prosperity will be yours.
3 Your wife will be like a fruitful vine within your house;
   your sons will be like olive shoots around your table.
4 Thus is the man blessed who fears the LORD.
5 May the LORD bless you from Zion all the days of
   your life; may you see the prosperity of Jerusalem,
6 and may you live to see your children's children.
   Peace upon Israel.

145

New International Version

from Letters to a Young Poet

RAINER MARIA RILKE

Marriage is in many ways a simplification of life, and it naturally combines the strengths and wills of two young people so that, together, they seem to reach farther into the future than they did before. Above all, marriage is a new task and a new seriousness – a new demand on the strength and generosity of each partner, and a great new danger for both.

The point of marriage is not to create a quick commonality by tearing down all boundaries; on the contrary, a good marriage is one in which each partner appoints the other to be the guardian of his solitude, and thus each shows the other the greatest possible trust. A merging of two people is an impossibility, and where it seems to exist, it is a hemming-in, a mutual consent that robs one party or both parties of their fullest freedom and development. But once the realisation is accepted that even between the closest people infinite distances exist, a marvellous living side-by-side can grow up for them, if they succeed in loving the expanse between them, which gives them a possibility of always seeing each other as a whole and before an immense sky...

Rainer Maria Rilke (1875–1926) was an Austrian lyric poet. Letters to a Young Poet *consists of 10 letters written to a young man considering entering the German army. These letters address personal issues and their span is tremendous covering topics including atheism, loneliness, sexuality and career.*

from Letters to a Young Poet

RAINER MARIA RILKE

Letter 7, Rome, 14 May 1904

...For one human being to love another: that is perhaps the most difficult of all tasks, the ultimate task, the final test and proof, the work for which all other work is merely preparation.

Love is at first not anything that means merging, surrendering, and uniting with another (for what purpose would a union of something unclarified serve?), rather it is high inducement to the individual to

Ripen, to become something in ourselves, to become a world in ourselves for the sake of another person. Love is a great, demanding claim on us, something that chooses us and calls us to vast distances.

POEM

from Love Song

RAINER MARIA RILKE

Everything that touches us, me and you,
takes us together like a violin's bow,
which draws one voice out of two
separate strings
Upon what instrument are we two spanned?
And what musician holds us in his hand?
Oh sweetest song.

What is Love?

WALTER RINDER

Love is just not looking at each other and saying
'You're wonderful'
There are times when we are anything but wonderful.

Love is looking out in the same direction, it is linking our
strength to pull a common load, it is pushing together
towards the far horizons, hand in hand.

Love is knowing that when our strength falters, we can
borrow the strength of someone who cares. Love is a
strange awareness that our sorrows will be shared and
made lighter by sharing; that joys will be enriched and
multiplied by the joy of another.

Love is knowing someone else cares that we are not alone in life.

Walter Rinder (b.1933) is an American humanist poet, philosopher and photographer, whose books of inspirational poetry on love reached the height of their popularity in the 1960s and 70s.

POEM

Credo

MATTHEW ROHRER

I believe there is something else

entirely going on but no single
person can ever know it,
so we fall in love.

It could also be true that what we use
everyday to open cans was something
much nobler, that we'll never recognise.

I believe the woman sleeping beside me
doesn't care about what's going on
outside, and her body is warm
with trust
which is a great beginning.

Matthew Rohrer (b. 1970) is an American poet. He has published several collections of poems, including Satellite *and* A Hummock in the Malookas.

Epithalamium

POEM

MATTHEW ROHRER

In the middle garden is the secret wedding,
that hides always under the other one
and under the shiny things of the other one.
Under a tree one hand reaches
through the grainy dusk toward another.
Two right hands.
The ring is a weed that will surely die.

There is no one else for miles,
and even those people far away are deaf and blind.
There is no one to bless this.
There are the dark trees, and just beyond the trees.

A Birthday

CHRISTINA ROSSETTI

My heart is like a singing bird
Whose nest is in a watered shoot;
My heart is like an apple tree
Whose boughs are bent with thickset fruit;
My heart is like a rainbow shell
That paddles in a halcyon sea;
My heart is gladder than all these
Because my love is come to me.

Raise me a dais of silk and down;
Hang it with vair and purple dyes;
Carve it in doves, and pomegranates,
And peacocks with a hundred eyes;
Work it in gold and silver grapes,
In leaves, and silver fleurs-de-lys;
Because the birthday of my life
Is come, my love is come to me.

*Christina Rossetti (1830–1894) came from a highly talented family
and is viewed as one of the most important female poets of 19th-century England.
She was a devout evangelical Christian and her poetry is mainly devotional or
for children.*

Reading

JALALUD'DIN RUMI

The minute I heard my first love story
I started looking for you,
not knowing how blind that was.
Lovers don't finally meet somewhere.
They're in each other all along.

Jalalud'din Rumi (1207–1273) was a 13th-century philosopher, mystic, scholar, poet and founder of the Whirling Dervishes, also known as the Mevlevi Order or Sufis, a spiritual offshoot of Islam. His poetry centres on the themes of tolerance, goodness, the experience of God, charity and awareness through love.

Prayer

ST FRANCIS OF ASSISI

Lord, make me an instrument of your peace,
Where there is hatred, let me sow love;
where there is injury, pardon;
where there is doubt, faith;
where there is despair, hope;
where there is darkness, light;
where there is sadness, joy;

O Divine Master, grant that I may not so much seek to be
consoled as to console;
to be understood as to understand;
to be loved as to love.

For it is in giving that we receive;
it is in pardoning that we are pardoned;
and it is in dying that we are born to eternal life.

St. Francis of Assisi (1182–1226) was born into a wealthy merchant family and enjoyed an extravagant youth before he underwent a conversion and devoted himself to God. He spent the rest of his life helping the poor, preaching, praying and serving God. His prayer has become one of the best-loved Christian prayers.

Untitled

POEM

CARL SANDBURG

I love you. I love you for what you are,
but I love you yet more for what you are going to be.
I love you not so much for your realities as for your ideals.
I pray for your desires, that they may be great,
rather than for your satisfactions,
which may be so hazardously little.
A satisfied flower is one whose petals are about to fall.
But the most beautiful rose is one,
hardly more than a bud,
wherein the pangs and ecstasies of desire are working for larger
and finer growth.
Not always shall you be what you are now.
You are going forward toward something great.
I am on the way with you and ... I love you.

Carl Sandburg (1878–1967) was an American poet, novelist, historian and folklorist. He won two Pulitzer prizes in his lifetime.

POEM

Under the Harvest Moon

CARL SANDBURG

Under the harvest moon,
When the soft silver
Drips shimmering
Over garden nights,
Death, the gray mocker,
Comes and whispers to you
As a beautiful friend
Who remembers.

Under the summer roses
When the flagrant crimson
Lurks in the dusk
Of the wild red leaves,
Love, with little hands,
Comes and touches you
With a thousand memories,
And asks you
Beautiful, unanswerable questions.

Two Fragments

S A P P H O

Love holds me captive again
and I tremble with bittersweet longing

As a gale on the mountainside bends the oak tree
I am rocked by my love

Sappho (c. 610–c. 580 BC) was an Ancient Greek poet from the island of Lesbos, a cultural centre in the 7th-century BC. She was a lyric poet who was noted for her themes of individual human experience. Unfortunately, only fragments of her work remain, of which the above are two.

PLAY

from Twelfth Night*

WILLIAM SHAKESPEARE

O Mistress mine, where are you roaming?
O, stay and hear; your true love's coming,
That can sing both high and low:
Trip no further, pretty sweeting;
Journeys end in lovers meeting,
Every wise man's son doth know.

... What is love? 'Tis not hereafter;
Present mirth hath present laughter;
What's to come is still unsure:
In delay there lies not plenty;
Then, come kiss me, sweet and twenty,
Youth's a stuff will not endure.

158
_____

* Clown, Act II, Scene iii

William Shakespeare (1564–1616), playwright and poet, has had his work studied more than that of any other author writing in the English language. He was rare as a playwright for excelling in tragedies, comedies and histories. Shakespeare has left a profound and lasting effect on Western culture.

from Romeo and Juliet[*]

WILLIAM SHAKESPEARE

My bounty is as boundless as the sea,
My love as deep; the more I give to thee,
The more I have, for both are infinite.

[*] Juliet to Romeo, Act II, Scene ii

from Hamlet[*]

WILLIAM SHAKESPEARE

Doubt thou the stars are fire;
Doubt that the sun doth move;
Doubt truth to be a liar;
But never doubt I love.

[*]Lord Polonius, Act II, Scene ii

POEM

Sonnet 18

WILLIAM SHAKESPEARE

Shall I compare thee to a summer's day?
Thou art more lovely and more temperate:
Rough winds do shake the darling buds of May,
And summer's lease hath all too short a date:
Sometime too hot the eye of heaven shines,
And often is his gold complexion dimmed;
And every fair from fair sometimes declines,
By chance, or nature's changing course, untrimmed;
But thy eternal summer shall not fade,
Nor lose possession of that fair thou owest,
Nor shall death brag thou wander'st in his shade,
When in eternal lines to time thou growest;
So long as men can breathe, or eyes can see,
So long lives this, and this gives life to thee.

Sonnet 116

POEM

WILLIAM SHAKESPEARE

Let me not to the marriage of true minds
Admit impediments. Love is not love
Which alters when it alteration finds,
Or bends with the remover to remove;
O, no, it is an ever-fixed mark,
That looks on tempests and is never shaken;
It is the star to every wandering bark,
Whose worth's unknown, although his height be taken.

Love's not Time's fool, though rosy lips and cheeks
Within his bending sickle's compass come;
Love alters not with his brief hours and weeks,
But bears it out even to the edge of doom.
If this be error and upon me proved,
I never writ, nor no man ever lov'd.

161

POEM

The Indian Serenade

PERCY BYSSHE SHELLEY

I arise from dreams of thee
In the first sweet sleep of night,
When the winds are breathing low,
And the stars are shining bright.
I arise from dreams of thee,
And a spirit in my feet
Has led me – who knows how? –
To thy chamber-window, sweet!

The wandering airs they faint
On the dark, the silent stream, –
The champak odors fail
Like sweet thoughts in a dream;
The nightingale's complaint,
It dies upon her heart,
As I must die on thine,
O, beloved as thou art!

O, lift me from the grass!
I die, I faint, I fail!
Let thy love in kisses rain
On my lips and eyelids pale.
My cheek is cold and white, alas!
My heart beats loud and fast:
Oh! press it close to thine again,
Where it will break at last!

Percy Bysshe Shelley (1792–1822) was one of the main contributors to the Romantic Movement. He eloped twice in his lifetime, first aged 19, and later with Mary Godwin Wollstoncraft, an intellectual who wrote the novel Frankenstein. *They lived as lovers in Switzerland with Lord Byron.*

Love's Philosophy

PERCY BYSSHE SHELLEY

The fountains mingle with the rivers
And the rivers with the oceans,
The winds of heaven mix forever
With a sweet emotion;
Nothing in the world is single;
All things by law divine
In one spirit meet and mingle.
Why not I with thine?

See the mountains kiss high heaven
And the waves clasp one another;
No sister-flower would be forgiven
If it disdained its brother,
And the sunlight clasps the earth
And the moonbeams kiss the sea:
What is all this sweet work worth
If thou kiss not me?

My True Love Hath my Heart and I Have His

SIR PHILIP SIDNEY

My true love hath my heart and I have his.
By just exchange one for the other given.
I hold his dear, and mine he cannot miss,
There never was a better bargain driven.
My true love hath my heart and I have his.
His heart in me keeps me and him in one,
My heart in him his thoughts and senses guides:
He loves my heart, for once it was his own,
I cherish his because in me it bides.
My true love hath my heart and I have his.

Sir Philip Sidney (1554–1586) was an English poet and patron of other poets. A firm Protestant, his work was never published in his lifetime as he avoided commercialism. He attended the court of Elizabeth I and upon his death, the Queen mourned the man who had exemplified the ideal courtier.

My Lover Spoke and Said to Me

SONG OF SOLOMON 2:10-13

10 My lover spoke and said to me,
   'Arise, my darling, my beautiful one,
   and come with me.
11 See! The winter is past;
   the rains are over and gone.
12 Flowers appear on the earth;
   the season of singing has come,
   the cooing of doves is heard in our land.
13 The fig tree forms its early fruit;
   the blossoming vines spread their fragrance.
   Arise, come, my darling;
   my beautiful one, come with me.'

New International Version

PRAYER

Wedding Prayer

ROBERT LOUIS STEVENSON

Lord, behold our family here assembled.
We thank you for this place in which we dwell,
for the love that unites us,
for the peace accorded us this day,
for the hope with which we expect the morrow,
for the health, the work, the food,
and the bright skies that make our lives delightful;
for our friends in all parts of the earth.

Amen.

Robert Louis Stevenson (1850–1894) was a Scottish essayist, poet and author of fiction and travel books, known especially for his adventure novels. His writing is varied, ranging from children's stories and poems, including Treasure Island *and* Kidnapped, *to* The Strange Case of Doctor Jekyll and Mr Hyde.

My Polar Star

POEM

RABINDRANATH TAGORE

I have made You the polar star of my
existence; never again can I lose my way in the
voyage of life.

Wherever I go, You are always there to
shower your benefience all around me. Your face
is ever present before my mind's eyes.

If I lose sight of You even for a moment, I
almost lose my mind.

Whenever my heart is about to go astray, just
a glance of You makes it feel ashamed of itself.

*Rabindranath Tagore (1861–1941) was an Indian poet and philosopher.
He received the Nobel Prize in literature in 1913 and was knighted in 1915,
an honour from which he resigned three years later in protest against British
policy in the Punjab.*

POEM

My Song

RABINDRANATH TAGORE

This song of mine will wind its music around you,
my child, like the fond arms of love.

The song of mine will touch your forehead
like a kiss of blessing.

When you are alone it will sit by your side and
whisper in your ear, when you are in the crowd
it will fence you about with aloofness.

My song will be like a pair of wings to your dreams,
it will transport your heart to the verge of the unknown.

It will be like the faithful star overhead
when dark night is over your road.

My song will sit in the pupils of your eyes,
and will carry your sight into the heart of things.

And when my voice is silenced in death,
my song will speak in your living heart.

Unending Love

POEM

RABINDRANATH TAGORE

I seem to have loved you in numberless forms, numberless times...
In life after life, in age after age, forever.
My spellbound heart has made and remade the necklace of songs,
That you take as a gift, wear round your neck in your many forms,
In life after life, in age after age, forever.

Whenever I hear old chronicles of love, it's age old pain,
It's ancient tale of being apart or together.
As I stare on and on into the past, in the end you emerge,
Clad in the light of a pole-star, piercing the darkness of time.
You become an image of what is remembered forever.

You and I have floated here on the stream that brings from the
fount.
At the heart of time, love of one for another.
We have played along side millions of lovers,
Shared in the same shy sweetness of meeting,
the distressful tears of farewell,
Old love but in shapes that renew and renew forever.

Love

PIERRE TEILHARD DE CHARDIN

Only love can bring individual beings to their perfect completion, as individuals, by uniting them one with another, because only love takes possession of them and unites them by what lies deepest within them. This is simply a fact of our everyday experience. For indeed at what moment do lovers come into the most complete possession of themselves if not when they say that they are lost in one another? And is not love all the time achieving – in couples, in teams, all around us – the magical and reputedly contradictory feat of personalising through totalising? And why should not what is thus daily achieved on a small scale be repeated one day on world-wide dimensions?

170

Humanity, the spirit of the earth, the synthesis of individuals and peoples, the paradoxical conciliation of the element with the whole, of the one with the many: all these are regarded as utopian fantasies, yet they are biologically necessary; and if we would see them made flesh in the world what more need we do than imagine our power to love growing and broadening, till it can embrace the totality of human beings and of the earth?

Pierre Teilhard de Chardin (1881–1955) was a French Jesuit theologian, palaeontologist and philosopher. He combined his scientific and spiritual beliefs, arguing that humanity is in a continuous process of evolution towards a perfect spiritual state.

Songs from the Princess

POEM

A L F R E D ,   L O R D   T E N N Y S O N

Now sleeps the crimson petal, now the white;
Nor waves the cypress in the palace walk;
Nor winks the gold fin in the porphyry font;
The fire-fly wakens: waken thou with me.

Now droops the milkwhite peacock like a ghost,
And like a ghost she glimmers on to me.
Now likes the Earth all Danae to the stars,
And all thy heart lies open unto me.

Now slides the silent meteor on, and leaves
A shining furrow, as thy thoughts in me.

Now folds the lily all her sweetness up,
And slips into the bosom of the lake:
So fold thyself, my dearest, thou, and slip
Into my bosom and be lost in me.

Alfred, Lord Tennyson (1809–1892) was perhaps the most popular poet of the Victorian period. He succeeded William Wordsworth as Poet Laureate in 1850 and the entire nation from Queen Victoria down paid homage to him. He was described by T. S. Eliot as 'the great master of metric as well as of melancholia'.

from Imitatio Christi

THOMAS À KEMPIS

Love is a mighty power, a great and complete good.
Love alone lightens every burden, and makes rough places
smooth.
It bears every hardship as though it were nothing, and renders
all bitterness sweet and acceptable.

Nothing is sweeter than love,
Nothing stronger,
Nothing higher,
Nothing wider,
Nothing more pleasant,
Nothing fuller or better in heaven or earth; for love is born
of God.

Love flies, runs and leaps for joy,
It is free and unrestrained.
Love knows no limits, but ardently transcends all bounds.
Love feels no burden, takes no account of toil,
Attempts things beyond its strength.

Love sees nothing as impossible,
for it feels able to achieve all things.
It is strange and effective,
while those who lack love faint and fail.

Love is not fickle and sentimental,
nor is it intent on vanities.
Like a living flame and a burning torch,
it surges upward and surely surmounts every obstacle.

Thomas à Kempis (1379–1471) was a Dutch Roman Catholic monk whose Imitatio Christi, *an instruction on how to love God, has become a classic.*

A Marriage

MARK TWAIN

POEM

A marriage
Makes of two fractional lives
A whole
It gives to two purposeless lives
A work, and doubles the strength
Of each to perform it
It gives to two
Questioning natures
A reason for living
And something to live for
It will give a new gladness
To the sunshine
A new fragrance to the flowers
A new beauty to the earth
And a new mystery to life.

Mark Twain (1835–1910) was born in Florida, Missouri, as Samuel Langhorne Clemens. He is most famous for the books that are drawn from his boyhood experiences: Tom Sawyer *and* Huckleberry Finn *both give vivid accounts of life on the Mississippi frontier.*

POEM

Love Song for Alex

MARGARET WALKER

My monkey-wrench man is my sweet patootie;
the lover of my life, my youth and age.
My heart belongs to him and to him only;
the children of my flesh are his and bear his rage
Now grown to years advancing through the dozens
the honeyed kiss, the lips of wine and fire
fade blissfully into the distant years of yonder
but all my days of Happiness and wonder
are cradled in his arms and eyes entire.
They carry us under the waters of the world
out past the starposts of a distant planet
And creeping through the seaweed of the ocean
they tangle us with ropes and yarn of memories
where we have been together, you and I.

Margaret Walker (1915–1998) is best known for her neo-slave narrative Jubilee *and the poem 'For My People'. She has received numerous awards for her work.*

The Most Wonderful of All Things in Life

SIR HUGH WALPOLE

The most wonderful of all things in life,
I believe, is the discovery of another human
being with whom one's relationship has a
growing depth, beauty and joy as the years
increase. This inner progressiveness of
love between two human beings is a most
marvellous thing; it cannot be found by
looking for it or by passionately wishing
for it. It is a sort of divine accident, and
the most wonderful of all things in life.

*Sir Hugh Walpole (1884–1941) was a New Zealand-born novelist. He
lived in Cumbria, England, for a considerable part of his life, where he was part of
a literary community. His books were hugely popular during his lifetime. He is
recognised for his descriptive powers and ability to evoke atmosphere.*

from Song of the Open Road

WALT WHITMAN

Listen! I will be honest with you,
I do not offer the old smooth prizes, but
Offer rough new prizes,
These are the days that must happen to you:
You shall not heap up what is call'd riches,
You shall scatter with lavish hand all that you earn or achieve.

However sweet these laid-up stores,
however convenient this dwelling, we cannot remain there.

However shelter'd the port, and however
calm the waters, we must not anchor here,
however welcome the hospitality that
surrounds us we are permitted to receive
it but a little while.

Afoot and light-hearted I take to the open road,
Healthy, free, the world before me,
The long brown path before me leading
Wherever I choose.

Camerado, I give you my hand!
I give you my love more precious than money,
I give you myself before preaching or law;
Will you give me yourself? Will you come
Travel with me?
Shall we stick by each other as long as we live?

Walt Whitman (1819–1892) was a groundbreaking American poet. His work celebrates love and Whitman caused much controversy with his vivid descriptions of homosexual love and the human form.

from A Love Letter

READING

MARY WOLLSTONECRAFT TO
WILLIAM GODWIN

4 October 1796

I would have liked to have dined with you today, after finishing your
essay – that my eyes, and lips, I do not exactly mean my voice, might
have told you that they had raised you in my esteem. What a cold
word! I would say love, if you will promise not to dispute about its
propriety, when I want to express an increasing affection, founded
on a more intimate acquaintance with your heart and understanding.

I shall cork up all my kindness – yet the fine volatile essence may fly
off in my walk – you know not how much tenderness for you may
escape in a voluptuous sigh, should the air, as is often the case, give
a pleasurable movement to the sensations, that have been clustering
round my heart, as I read this morning – reminding myself, every
now and then, that the writer loved me.

177

Voluptuous is often expressive of a meaning I do not now intend to
give, I would describe one of those moments, when the senses are
exactly tuned by the ringing tenderness of the heart and according
reason entices you to live in the present moment, regardless of the
past or future – it is not rapture – it is sublime tranquility.

I have felt it in your arms – hush! Let not the light see, I was going to
say hear it – these confessions should only be uttered – you know
where, when the curtains are up – and all the world shut out – Ah me!

I wish I may find you at home when I carry this letter to drop it in the
box, – that I may drop a kiss with it into your heart, to be embalmed,
till me meet, closer.

*Mary Wollstonecraft (1819–1892) was an Anglo-Irish feminist and writer.
She wrote this to philosopher and writer William Godwin, whom she married
on 29 March, 1797.*

POEM

Perfect Woman

WILLIAM WORDSWORTH

She was a phantom of delight
When first she gleam'd upon my sight;
A lovely apparition, sent
To be a moment's ornament;
Her eyes as stars of twilight fair;
Like twilight's, too, her dusky hair;
But all things else about her drawn
From May-time and the cheerful dawn;
A dancing shape, an image gay,
To haunt, to startle, and waylay.

I saw her upon nearer view,
A spirit, yet a Woman too!
Her household motions light and free,
And steps of virgin liberty;
A countenance in which did meet
Sweets records, promises as sweet;
A creature not too bright or good
For human natures daily food;
For transient sorrows, simple wiles,
Praise, blame, love, kisses, tears, and smiles.

And now I see with eye serene
The very pulse of the machine;
A being breathing thoughtful breath,
A traveller between life and death;

The reason firm, the temperate will,
Endurance, foresight, strength, and skill;
A perfect woman, nobly plann'd,
To warn, to comfort, and command;
And yet a Spirit still, and bright
With something of angelic light.

William Wordsworth (1770–1850) was credited with ushering in the English Romantic Movement with the publication of Lyrical Ballads (1798), in collaboration with Samuel Taylor Coleridge. Wordsworth wrote poetry that explored nature, which was viewed as divine.

He Wishes for the Cloths of Heaven

W.B. YEATS

Had I the heavens' embroidered cloths,
Enwrought with golden and silver light,
The blue and the dim and the dark cloths
Of night and light and the half-light,
I would spread the cloths under your feet:
But I, being poor, have only my dreams;
I have spread my dreams under your feet;
Tread softly because you tread on my dreams.

W. B. Yeats (1865–1939) was one of the founders of the Irish Literary Revival. His poetry draws upon Irish myth and legend and a glorified image of the peasant. He won the Nobel Prize for Literature in 1923.

The Lover Tells of the Rose in his Heart

POEM

W.B. YEATS

All things uncomely and broken, all things worn out and old,
The cry of a child by the roadway, the creak of a lumbering cart,
The heavy steps of the ploughman, splashing the wintry mould,
Are wronging your image that blossoms a rose in the deeps of
my heart.

The wrong of unshapely things is a wrong too great to be told;
I hunger to build them anew and sit on a green knoll apart,
With the earth and the sky and the water, re-made, like a
casket of gold
For my dreams of your image that blossoms a rose in the
deeps of my heart.

When You Are Old

W.B. YEATS

When you are old and grey and full of sleep,
And nodding by the fire, take down this book,
And slowly read, and dream of the soft look
Your eyes had once, and of their shadows deep;

How many loved your moments of glad grace,
And loved your beauty with love false or true,
But one man loved the pilgrim Soul in you,
And loved the sorrows of your changing face;

And bending down beside the glowing bars,
Murmur, a little sadly, how Love fled
And paced upon the mountains overhead
And hid his face amid a crowd of stars.

Short Quotations
on Love and Marriage

'Like everything which is not the involuntary result of fleeting emotion but the creation of time and will, any marriage, happy or unhappy, is infinitely more interesting than any romance, however passionate.'
– W. H. Auden, poet (1907–1973)

'A lady's imagination is very rapid; it jumps from admiration to love, from love to matrimony in a moment.'
– Jane Austen (1775–1817)

'Love does not begin and end the way we seem to think it does. Love is a battle, love is a war; love is a growing up.'
– James A. Baldwin, writer (1924–1987)

'When the one man loves the one woman and the one woman loves the one man, the very angels desert heaven and sit in that hour and sing for joy ...'
– Brahma-Sutra

'Grow old along with me; the best is yet to be.'
– Robert Browning, writer (1812–1889)

'A good marriage is one which allows for change and growth in the individuals and in the way they express their love.'
– Pearl Buck, novelist (1892–1973)

'God is Love – I dare say. But what a mischievous devil Love is!'
– Samuel Butler, satirist (1612–1680)

'Never love unless you can bear with all the faults of man!'
– Thomas Campion, physician, poet and composer (1567–1620)

'Perhaps the feelings that we experience when we are in love represent a normal state. Being in love shows a person who he should be.'
– Anton Chekhov, writer (1860–1904)

'An archaeologist is the best husband any woman can have: the older she gets, the more interested he is in her.'
– Agatha Christie, writer (1891–1975)

'Love does not consist of gazing at each other, but looking outward in the same direction.'
– Antoine de Saint–Exupery, writer (1900–1944)

'If there is such a thing as a good marriage, it is because it resembles friendship rather than love.'
– Michel de Montaigne, writer (1533–1592)

'Absence diminishes small loves and increases great ones, as the wind blows out the candle and blows up the bonfire.'
– François de la Rouchefoucauld, writer (1613–1680)

'The only gift is a portion of thyself.'
– Ralph Waldo Emerson, writer (1803–1882)

'If you want to be loved, love and be lovable.'
– Benjamin Franklin, statesman (1706–1790)

'Love is an irresistible desire to be irresistibly desired.'
– Robert Frost, poet (1874 – 1963)

'There is nothing nobler or more admirable than when two people who see eye to eye keep house as man and wife, confounding their enemies and delighting their friends.'
– Homer, writer (c. 8th century BC)

'We come to love not by finding the perfect person, but by learning to see an imperfect person perfectly.'
– Angelina Jolie, actor (b. 1975)

'I first learned the concepts of non-violence in my marriage.'
– Mahatma Gandhi, spiritual leader (1869–1948)

'Where there is love there is life.'
– Mahatma Gandhi

'You are always new, The last of your kisses was ever the sweetest.'
– John Keats, poet (1795–1821)

'Being deeply loved by someone gives you strength; loving someone deeply gives you courage.'
– Lao Tzu (c. 600 BC)

'We've got this gift of love, but love is like a precious plant. You can't just accept it and leave it in the cupboard or just think it's going to get on by itself. You've got to keep watering it. You've got to really look after it and nurture it.'
– John Lennon, singer and musician (1940–1980)

'Rituals are important. Nowadays it's hip not to be married. I'm not interested in being hip.'
– John Lennon

*'To be brave is to love someone unconditionally,
without expecting anything in return. To just give.
That takes courage, because we don't want to fall
on our faces or leave ourselves open to hurt'.*
– Madonna, musician (b. 1958)

*'A marriage without conflicts is almost as inconceivable
as a nation without crises.'*
– André Maurois, writer (1885–1967)

*'The best friend is likely to acquire the best wife, because a
good marriage is based on the talent for friendship.'*
– Friedrich Nietzsche, philosopher and writer (1844–1900)

*'Love is the joy of the good, the wonder of the wise,
the amazement of the Gods.'*
– Plato, philosopher (c. 428–348 BC)

'Spice a dish with love and it pleases every palate.'
– Plautus, Roman dramatist (c. 254–184 BC)

'I love thee like puddings; if thou wert pie I'd eat thee.'
– John Ray, naturalist (1627–1705)

*'There is only one happiness in life,
to love and be loved'.*
– George Sands, writer (1804–1876)

'Love looks not with the eyes, but with the mind...'
– William Shakespeare, dramatist, poet (1564–1616)

'If music be the food of love, play on...'
– William Shakespeare

*'By all means marry. If you get a good wife you
will become happy, and if you get a bad one
you will become a philosopher.'*
– Socrates, philosopher (469–399 BC)

*'One word frees us of all the weight and pain
of life; that word is love.'*
– Sophocles, philosopher (c. 496–406 BC)

'And all for love, and nothing for reward.'
– Edmund Spenser, writer (1552–1599)

'There is no remedy for love than to love more.'
– Henry David Thoreau, philosopher, writer (1817–1862)

*'A successful man is one who can make
more money than his wife can spend.
A successful woman is one who can
find such a man.'*
– Lana Turner, actor (1920–1995)

*'When you fish for love, bait with your heart,
not your brain.'*
– Mark Twain, writer (1835–1910)

'Love those who love you.'
– Voltaire, writer, philosopher (1694–1778)

'Marriage is the triumph of imagination over intelligence.'
– Oscar Wilde, poet and dramatist (1854–1900)

'I married beneath me, all women do!'
– W. B. Yeats (1865–1939)

Acknowledgements

Every effort has been made to contact copyright holders, but should there be any omissions, New Holland Publishers would be pleased to insert the appropriate acknowledgement in any subsequent printing of this publication.

Extract from *A Natural History of Love* by Diane Ackerman, copyright © 1994 by Diane Ackerman. Used by permission of Random House, Inc. 'Come. And Be My Baby' from *Oh Pray My Wings Are Gonna Fit Me Well* by Maya Angelou. Copyright © 1975 by Maya Angelou, Used by permission of Random House, Inc; In the UK: reprinted by permission of Virago, an imprint of Little, Brown Book Group. 'Habitation' by Margaret Atwood; in the British Commonwealth from *Procedures for Underground* Copyright © Margaret Atwood 1970 reproduced with permission of Curtis Brown Group Ltd, London. In the US from *Selected Poems*, 1965–1975. Copyright © 1976 by Margaret Atwood. Reprinted by permission of Houghton Mifflin Harcourt Publishing Company. All rights reserved. 'Lullaby' and 'O Tell Me the Truth About Love' from *Collected Poems* by W. H. Auden, edited by Edward Mendelson, reprinted by permission of Faber and Faber Ltd. 'Yes, I'll Marry You, My Dear' from *With These Hands* by Pam Ayres, published by Weidenfeld and Nicolson, Copyright © 1997 Pam Ayres, is reproduced by permission of Sheil Land Associates Ltd. Extract from *Captain Corelli's Mandolin* by Louis de Bernières, published by Vintage. Reprinted by permission of The Random House Group Ltd. In the US: copyright © 1994 by Louis de Bernières. Used by permission of Pantheon Books, a division of Random House, Inc. 'A Wedding Sermon from a Prison Cell' by Dietrich Bonhoeffer from *Letters And Papers From Prison* reproduced by permission of SCM-Canterbury Press Ltd. In the US: reprinted with the permission of Scribner, a Division of Simon & Schuster, Inc., from *Letters And Papers From Prison*, Enlarged Ed. by Dietrich Bonhoeffer. Copyright © 1953, 1967, 1971 by SCM Press Ltd. All rights reserved. 'Sermon at Rajagaha verses 19-22' from *The Gospel of Buddha* by Paul Carus. Reprinted by permission of Open Court Publishing Company, a division of Carus Publishing Company, Peru, IL. Copyright © 2004 by Carus Publishing. 'After the Lunch' by Wendy Cope: in the UK from *Two Cures For Love: Selected Poems 1979-2006*, Reprinted by permission of Faber and Faber Ltd. In North America and Canada: 'After the Lunch' from *Serious Concerns* by Wendy Cope reprinted by permission of United Agents on behalf of: Wendy Cope. 'i carry your heart with me(i carry it in' is reprinted from *Complete Poems 1904-1952*, by E.E. Cummings, edited by George J. Firmage, by permission of W.W Norton & Company. Copyright © 1991 by the Trustees for the E.E. Cummings Trust and George James Firmage. 'i love you much(most beautiful darling) is reprinted from *Complete Poems 1904-1952*, by E.E. Cummings, edited by George J. Firmage, by permission of W.W Norton & Company. Copyright © 1991 by the Trustees for the E.E. Cummings Trust and George James Firmage. 'I Will be There' by Stephen Curtis Chapman reproduced by permission of Small Stone Media, Copyright © 1990 Careers BMG Music / Greg Nelson Music / Sparrow Song, USA (adm. in Europe by Small Stone Media, Holland). Extract from *The Divine Comedy* by Dante Alighieri, translated by C.H. Sisson reproduced by permission of Pollinger Limited and The Estate of C.H. Sisson. 'Song' from *The Complete Poems* by C Day Lewis published by Sinclair-Stevenson (1992) Copyright © 1992 in this edition The Estate of C Day Lewis. Reprinted by permission of The Random House Group Ltd. 'Hope is the Thing With Feathers' and 'Wild Night! Wild Nights!' reprinted by permission of the publishers and the Trustees of Amherst College from *ThePoems of Emily Dickinson*, Thomas H. Johnson, ed., Cambridge Mass.: The Belknap Press of Harvard University Pres, Copyright © 1951, 1955, 1979, 1983 by the President and Fellows of Harvard College. 'Blessing for a Marriage' by James Dillet Freeman reprinted by permission of Unity, www.unityonline.org. 'A Dedication to My Wife' from *Collected Poems 1909-1962* by T.S. Eliot. Reprinted by permission of Faber and Faber Ltd; In the US from *Collected Poems 1909-1962* by T.S. Eliot, copyright 1936 by Houghton Mifflin Harcourt Publishing Company and renewed 1964 by T.S. Eliot, reprinted by permission of Houghton Mifflin Harcourt Publishing Company. Extract from Robert Frost's 'The Master Speed' from *The Poetry of Robert Frost* edited by Edward Connery Lathem, published by Jonathan Cape. Reprinted by permission of The Random House Group Ltd. Extracts from 'On Children', 'On Friendship', 'On Love' and 'On Marriage' from *The*

Prophet by Kahlil Gibran, Copyright © 1923 and renewed 1951 by Administrators C.T.A. of Kahlil Gibran Estate and Mary G. Gibran. Used by permission of Alfred A. Knopf, a division of Random House, Inc. 'My Funny Valentine' Hart, Lorenz (A)/Rodgers, Richard (C) © 1937 (Renewed) Warner/Chappell Music Ltd (PRS) and Warner/Chappell Music Publishing Ltd (PRS). Extract from *A Farewell to Arms* by Ernest Hemmingway, published by Jonathan Cape. Reprinted by permission of The Random House Group Ltd. In the US and Canada reprinted with the permission of Scribner, a Division of Simon & Schuster, Inc. Copyright 1929 by Charles Scribner's Sons. Copyright renewed © 1957 by Ernest Hemingway. 'Lovesong' from *The Collected Poems of Ted Hughes* by Ted Hughes. Reprinted by permission of Faber and Faber Ltd. Extract from *The Complete I Ching* by Taoist Master Alfred Huang, Rochester, VT05767. Copyright © 1998 Inner Traditions. Reprinted by permission of Bear & Co. 'Wedding-Wind' from *Collected Poems* by Philip Larkin Hughes. Reprinted by permission of and Faber and Faber Ltd. Extract from 'Fidelity' from *The Complete Works of D.H. Lawrence* is reproduced by permission of Pollinger Limited and The Estate of Frieda Lawrence Ravagli. Extract from *A Gift from the Sea* by Anne Morrow Lindbergh, published by Chatto and Windus. Reprinted by permission of The Random House Group Ltd. In the US and Canada: copyright © 1955, 1975, renewed 1983 by Anne Morrow Lindbergh. Used by permission of Pantheon Books, a division of Random House, Inc. 'Tin Wedding Whistle' and 'Reprise' by Ogden Nash, Copyright © 1947 by Ogden Nash and Copyright © 1941 by Ogden Nash. Reprinted by permission of Curtis Brown. Sonnets IX, XLV XVII, XXVII from *100 Love Sonnets; Cien Sonetos de Amor* by Pablo Neruda, translated by Stephen Tapscott, Copyright © Pablo Neruda and Fundacion Pablo Neruda, Copyright © 1986 by the University of Texas Press. By permission of the University of Texas Press. 'We Have Lost Even' from *Twenty Love Songs and a Song of Despair* by Pablo Neruda, published by Jonathan Cape. Reprinted by permission of The Random House Group Ltd. 'Wedding' from *The Thing in the Gap Stone Stile* by Alice Oswald. Reprinted by permission of Faber and Faber Ltd. In North America and Canada reprinted by permission of United Agents on behalf of: Alice Oswald. Extract from *The Art of Marriage* by Wilferd Arlan Peterson, Souvenir Press. Copyright © Wilfred Arlan Peterson. In the US: Extract from 'The Art of Marriage', an essay by Wilferd A. Peterson (published in *The New Book of the Art of Living*, Simon & Schuster, New York, copyright Wilferd Arlan Peterson, 1962, 1963; copyright Lilian Thorpe, 2004). Permission granted by Dr. Peterson's estate representative, the Heacock Literary Agency, Inc. Extract from The Symposium from *Penguin Great Ideas: The Symposium* by Plato, translated by Christopher Gill (Penguin Classics, 2005). Copyright © Christopher Gill, 1999. Reproduced by permission of Penguin Books Ltd. 'Credo' and 'Epithalamium' from Satellite by Matthew Rohrer. Copyright © 2001 by Verse Press (now Wave Books). Reprinted with permission of Wave Books and the author. Rumi quotation from *Selected Poems: Rumi* translated by Coleman Banks (Penguin Books, 2004). Copyright © Coleman Banks, 1995. Reproduced by permission of Penguin Books Ltd. 'Under the Harvest Moon' from *Chicago Poems* by Carl Sandburg, copyright © 1916 by Holt, Rinehart and Winston and renewed 1944 by Carl Sandburg, reprinted by permission of Houghton Mifflin Harcourt Publishing Company. 'Unending Love' and 'My Song' by Rabindranath Tagore from *Rabindranath Tagore: Selected Poems* translated by William Radice (Penguin, 1985). Copyright © William Radice, 1985. 'My Polar Star' by Rabindranath Tagore from *Heart of God: Poems by Rabindranath Tagore* translated by Herbert Vetter, by permission of Tuttle Publishing, a member of the Periplus Publishing Group. Extract from *Hymn of the Universe* by Pierre Teilhard de Chardin. Copyright © 1961 by Editions du Seuil. English translation Copyright © 1965 by William Collins Sons & Co., Ltd., London and Harper & Row, Inc., New York. Reprinted by permission of Georges Borchardt, Inc., for Editions du Seuil. 'Love Song for Alex' by Margaret Walker from *This is my Century: New and Collected Poems*. Copyright © 1989 Margaret Walker Alexander. Reprinted by permission of The University of Georgia Press. 'He wishes for the Cloths of Heaven', 'The Lover Tells of the Rose in his Heart' and 'When You are Old' all by W.B. Yeats reproduced by permission of A.P. Watt Ltd on behalf of Grainne Yeats. Scripture quotations taken from the Holy Bible, *New International Version*. Copyright © 1973, 1978, 1984 by International Bible Society. Used by permission of Hodder & Stoughton Publishers, A member of the Hachette Livre UK Group. All rights reserved.

Index of First Lines